Psychology and Christianity: the view both ways

Malcolm A. Jeeves
M.A., PH.D., F.B.PS.S., F.A.P.S.
Professor of Psychology in the University of St Andrews

Inter-Varsity Press

© Inter-Varsity Press, Leicester, England

Universities and Colleges Christian Fellowship
38 De Montfort Street, Leicester LE1 7GP

First Edition July 1976

ISBN 0 85111 316 8

Printed in Great Britain by
Billing & Sons Limited
Guildford, London and Worcester

Psychology and Christianity:
the view both ways

Also by Malcolm A. Jeeves:

The Scientific Enterprise and Christian Faith

Based on the findings of a conference of research scientists, this book looks at determinism, cosmology, evolution and other ideas in modern science, and their impact on Christian beliefs.

Contents

Preface

Along with other social and behavioural sciences psychology is today widely taught in universities, colleges of education and similar tertiary institutions. The need to cover a wide range of subject-matter in a short course sometimes results in a lecture style which sounds excessively dogmatic. In such a situation, where there is not enough time to qualify every statement and discuss all the evidence for and against different theories, a student can understandably misinterpret some (to the lecturer) innocent statement and see it as conflicting with what he believes as a Christian. For example, the simple, factually accurate statement, that 'psychologists are able to offer explanations of conversion', is easily seen as diametrically opposed to the statement that 'conversion is the work of the Holy Spirit'.

On closer scrutiny, however, it sometimes turns out that supposed conflicts between what psychologists have discovered and what Christians believe have arisen through not pausing long enough to establish precisely what the psychologist is and is not asserting, and what a biblical faith does and does not encourage us to believe. One of the main aims of this book, therefore, is to show how Christian beliefs and the statements of behavioural scientists concerning the same set of events may be related, so that neither is abused and both are given full weight.

This, then, is not a book on the psychology of religion. It is about the relationship between what psychologists have discovered and what Christians believe. As we examine how these are related we shall need to discuss specific topics concerning the psychology of religion in order to illustrate the points being made. The particular issues included have been selected on the grounds that, in the author's experience, they are the ones which are most often raised with him by students as they reflect upon what is taught in psychology courses, or because students themselves have asked for them to be discussed. For example, every psychology student hears about Skinner, many hear about Freud, and most are told something about the biological bases of behaviour. At the same time few ever hear 'the nature of man' discussed in psychology lectures, any more than physics students hear 'the nature of the universe' discussed. Nevertheless, because 'the nature of man' is *not* discussed, it is therefore sometimes inferred that the psychologist assumes that man is nothing but a naked ape, a complex computer or a conditioned automaton. Often, though not always, such inferences are unjustified; but because they are not discussed they are dislodged only with difficulty.

The truth, I believe, is that both psychology and true religion are completely misinterpreted when cast in the roles of enemies rather than allies. In their different ways both have much to contribute to man's fulfilment and well-being. I hope that this small book will help to change attitudes of suspicion and, at times, of scarcely concealed hostility into ones of mutual respect. I believe that as Christians seek to understand what psychologists are saying and doing they face two temptations. The first is to construe psychological statements as necessarily in competition with religious statements when in fact they are complementary. The second temptation is to endow psychological statements with a finality which those who make them seldom intend. One result of this has been successive attempts to restate traditional Christian beliefs in the latest psychological jargon in the belief that in some way this makes them more acceptable to contemporary man. At times this has resulted in ingenious attempts to demonstrate that this or that latest psychological model of man fits with the Christian model, with a further implication that if we had been clever enough we could have found it all in Scripture anyway. Each of these temptations will be faced and discussed many times in what follows, as specific areas of apparent overlap of psychology and Christianity are examined. The issues raised will include the implications of psychological research for Christian beliefs about God, man, freedom, responsibility, sin, immortality, and so on. In our discussion of these issues we shall try to indicate a method of approach to the evaluation of psychological knowledge which can be applied to other issues not raised here as well as to those which will arise from the results of research still to be done.

Since Christian ministers are sometimes asked to help students worried by what they have learned in one or other of the behavioural sciences, I have tried to write this book so that it will help the non-specialist as well as the specialist. In order to do this I have made extensive use of footnotes. In these I suggest further reading for psychology students wishing to follow up particular issues in greater detail. Understandably, I have written about those aspects of behavioural science with which I am most familiar, namely, experimental psychology. Students specializing in other behavioural sciences such as sociology and anthropology should be able, without too much difficulty, to apply the lessons learned here to the particular problems which those subjects seem to generate for Christian beliefs.

I am grateful to all those students and colleagues who have influenced my thinking about psychology and Christianity. When, in response to student requests, I tried to set my views down on paper, I first produced something more like a manuscript for a scientific journal than a readable book. Such is the force of habit. However, the blunt comments of students and the more polite, though no less searching criticisms of colleagues soon changed all that. The extent to which what I have now produced is readable is due almost entirely to the untiring effort of Mr Ronald Inchley, Chairman of the Publications Committee of the Inter-Varsity Press. He has coaxed me, coached me and helped me to a degree far beyond anything that his official role required. I am delighted to record my great indebtedness to him now. The influence of my friend Professor Donald MacKay will be evident at many points. In addition to making helpful comments on an

earlier draft of the book he also kindly vetted the section where I
try to set out his views on logical indeterminacy.

St Andrews   MALCOLM JEEVES
April, 1976

1 Introduction

This small book is not primarily concerned with what psychologists have said about religion, nor even with what different people have written about how psychology and religion should be related. Rather, it tries to suggest how one should go about answering questions which arise as one seeks to relate what psychologists have discovered to what Christians believe and do. Inevitably, psychology of religion will be discussed as we get down to specific issues. We shall be concerned in the main, however, with relating what psychologists say about how religious people feel and act to what those same people say in their own religious language about the selfsame experience and behaviour. Because I am a Christian, I shall confine myself, almost exclusively, to considering what Christians believe and do. The reader who wishes to follow up in more detail what is written here on the psychology of religion may consult the references given in the footnotes.

Psychologists and their presuppositions
Like the members of any other profession, psychologists come from a wide variety of intellectual, social and cultural backgrounds. Some, like the present writer, were first trained in the natural sciences; others studied arts-type subjects, often including philosophy; yet others studied psychology along with other social sciences such as politics, sociology, economics. Understandably,

the influence of the different backgrounds is later reflected in any specialist research. But background and personal values not only influence psychologists' research interests; they also emerge, as with other scientists, in their more speculative writings.

In addition to these more general formative influences on what psychologists write, there are others which predispose them to favour one theoretical interpretation of the data over another. If your early training has been in physics and mathematics you will probably try to fit your data to a mathematical model. Psychology students will be familiar with information theory and signal-detection theory as examples of this kind of approach. If, on the other hand, you concentrate on studying how organisms respond to particular stimuli, deliberately refusing at the same time to refer to any unobservable processes within the organism, you will probably favour the approach championed by Skinner and his disciples. Alternatively, if you are deliberately concerned with what goes on inside the organism, you will study the physiological and chemical processes underlying learning. Or, you may prefer to try to account for both normal and abnormal behaviour in terms of the interplay of hypothetical entities such as the ego, the super-ego and the id, as Freudian psychologists have done.

Life would certainly be simpler if there were one theoretical framework to which all psychologists subscribed and which was so well developed and so precisely formulated that it could be unambiguously applied to explain all that people felt and did. Such, however, is not yet the case. In spite of this there have been some popularizers of psychology who have written as if the subject were a monolithic whole with an agreed and unified body of theory which is at variance with religious beliefs. One such was Freud. He not only believed that a conflict existed, but also seemed to believe that, ultimately, religion must be defeated and replaced by psychology which, in a scientific way, would do what religion has been trying to do in a fumbling, haphazard way down the centuries. Other writers do not take such an extreme point of view. Nevertheless, they give the impression that, if you can explain some aspects of religious behaviour psychologically, you have therefore explained them away, so that talking about the same events in religious language is either superfluous or false. For example, some who do this believe that to behave religiously expresses a basic immaturity, and that once people as individuals, or as groups, grow up, then they will be able to dispense with the childish beliefs associated with religion and be able to face the world in a more mature fashion.

Explaining and explaining away

In the light of what has just been said, it is not surprising that many people believe that, in some way, psychology has not only begun to explain religion but that ultimately it will explain it away completely. Such a view, however, is rarely found in the writings of professional psychologists. No doubt there are a number of reasons for this. Professional psychologists, especially those actively engaged in research, tend to have a much more modest estimate of what they have so far achieved, and would certainly hesitate to generalize or speculate too readily about the relevance, if any, of their present knowledge to so complex a phenomenon as religious experience and behaviour. If one asks what those who specialize in the psychology of religion have written one may turn to a standard, well-respected work of reference in psychology, such as, for example, the five-volume *Handbook of Social Psychology*. There we read in the chapter on the psychology of religion:

'Logically the distinction between the two disciplines seems clear. Though psychology and philosophy (and theology) may be concerned with the same phenomenon, such as a particular belief or a particular ritual, they are asking different questions about it. Psychology is concerned with such questions as the psychological history and function of the belief or rituals; philosophy is concerned with such questions as the truth or goodness of the belief or ritual. Judgements of the latter kind are based on their own criteria, and there is no clear logic by which the answers to the psychological questions can either imply or presuppose answers to the philosophical questions.'[1]

The same point is taken up in a recent book on Christianity and psychology by Professor A. T. Welford, who writes:

'The psychological and religious views of man that we have outlined, are not as fundamentally opposed as they appear at first sight to be. They differ mainly because they have been developed for different purposes. The psychological view presents a working hypothesis designed to co-ordinate the facts obtained from a large number of scientific studies and to guide the search for further facts. It is thus tentative, subject to frequent modification, and clearly incomplete in that it does not cover areas in which evidence is lacking. . . .'[2]

In view of the confusion over this simple yet basic point, it is justifiable, perhaps, to labour it a little and draw attention to another standard reference work which has just been published in its third edition. I refer to *An Introduction to the Psychology of Religion*[3] by Dr R. H. Thouless. The author points out how, during the last thirty or forty years, the number of enquiries into particular problems in religious psychology has been enormous, and that it is difficult now for any one book to attempt to deal with all of them. He suggests that there is much to be gained by theologians and clergy taking seriously the things that psychologists can say, both about religious behaviour and religious experience; yet at the same time he is extremely careful to indicate the confusion that arises the moment one imagines that giving an explanation of some aspect of religious behaviour in psychological terms is a substitute for one which may be given from a different standpoint in spiritual terms.

[1] Dittes, James E., 'The Psychology of Religion', chapter 44 in *Handbook of Social Psychology*, ed. Lindzey and Aronson, 2nd ed., Vol. 5 (Addison-Wesley, Reading, Mass., 1969).
[2] Welford, A. T., *Christianity – A Psychologist's Translation* (Hodder and Stoughton, London, 1971), p. 16.
[3] Thouless, R. H., *An Introduction to the Psychology of Religion*, 3rd ed. (CUP, London, 1971).

In another standard reference work in this field, published in 1958, Michael Argyle of Oxford puts this point much more bluntly and arrestingly when he writes:

'Audiences to whom I have talked about these matters have often been more concerned about the religious implications of the findings than about the findings themselves. This is all rather absurd; psychologists are no more experts on the existence of God than are theologians on the theory of learning or art critics on the nature of the atom. Psychologists have been diverted from their proper task – that of discovering the empirical generalizations or laws governing religious beliefs, behaviour and experiences, together with finding theories or mechanisms to explain these laws. The beliefs of the psychologist cannot affect his findings unless he actually cheats, so that there is no special kind of psychologist known as a "Christian psychologist" – that would simply be a psychologist who happens to hold Christian beliefs.'[4]

And shortly afterwards, he continues,

'We conclude that psychological research can tell us nothing about the truth, validity or usefulness of religious phenomena; these are questions which must be settled in other ways.'

Some readers may feel that, by selectively choosing my quotations, I have carefully ignored those psychologists who hold that, when religious behaviour is understood psychologically, there is nothing more of value to be said about it. Such an objector would no doubt have in mind what men like Dr William Sargant have written in books like *Battle for the Mind*[5] and, more recently, *The Mind Possessed*.[6] This is in spite of Dr Sargant's stating clearly that

---

[4] Argyle, M., *Religious Behaviour* (Routledge and Kegan Paul, London, 1958), p. 1.
[5] Sargant, W., *Battle for the Mind* (Heinemann, London, 1957).
[6] Sargant, W., *The Mind Possessed* (Heinemann, London, 1973).

'It must be emphasised as strongly as possible that this book is *not* concerned with the truth or falsity of any particular religious or political belief. Its purpose is to examine some of the mechanisms involved in the fixing or destroying of such beliefs in the human brain.'

And, finally, since the views of Professor B. F. Skinner are today widely studied by psychology students, it is perhaps worth noting that when he was cross-questioned on television about his views on religion he said,

'I am in no position to pronounce judgements on the effect that religion has had on our culture.'

A little later in the same programme, when speculating about how his psychological insights helped him to understand why people behaved religiously, he added,

'I am in no position to give you a complete account of religion any more than a complete account of anything else.'[7]

In continuing this brief introductory review it is perhaps worth noting how, in his chapter on the psychology of religion in the *Handbook of Social Psychology* already referred to, Dr Dittes mentioned that at least one-fourth of the Presidents of the American Psychological Association have given their attention to the study of religion at some point of their careers, and according to his calculations this rate persists about equally in every decade. This may come as a surprise to some psychology students, as it did to me, since it is widely believed that very few distinguished psychologists have been actively interested in studying religion. One wonders why so few have persisted with that interest. Possibly they have found it such a complex and uncharted field of study, with so many pitfalls, that they have withdrawn to areas where at least the issues can already be seen with some clarity, and where we have some techniques which hold out promise of giving limited answers to circumscribed problems.

[7] Skinner, B. F., in *Firing Line,* a transcript of a programme dated 17 October 1971.

Psychology and religion: some mutual concerns

I hope that no-one will be put off the psychological study of religion because in the past psychologists and theologians have been mistakenly cast in the roles of producing competing explanations of religious experience and behaviour. Indeed, I wish to argue that what we can learn from psychological research is extremely relevant as we try to understand what leads people to hold religious beliefs and to act religiously. That there is an urgent need for a scholarly and systematic application of our present psychological knowledge to the practice of religion is exemplified by the current trend in pastoral psychology. If this demand is not met by scholars with a detailed knowledge and balanced assessment of the strengths and weaknesses of current psychological theories, it will surely become a happy hunting-ground for well-meaning enthusiasts with more zeal than knowledge, and more concern for results than for truth. But the issues of mutual concern are too serious and go too deep to be left either to a small group of religious enthusiasts with a smattering of psychology, or to professional psychologists with minimal insight into the resources of true religion.

What sorts of issues do I have in mind? Consider three. Why do some of the more serious forms of mental illness often manifest themselves in the holding of bizarre religious ideas? In what ways do present-day enthusiasms for the benefit of group activities, variously referred to as encounter groups, sensitivity training or T-groups, represent a mid-twentieth-century rediscovery, in a non-religious context, of the blessings long known to small groups of Christians enjoying a true unity in Christ? How do religious beliefs emerge and develop in the thought and behaviour of a growing child, and what can psychology teach us about religious education? To answer any one of these questions would require a book larger than this one. They are mentioned here simply to show that there are problems of common concern to psychology and religion calling for careful, systematic study. We shall be saying something more about them later in this book as we deal with specific issues.

The plan of the book

I shall argue that there is no necessary conflict between the assured results of psychological researches into religious behaviour and experience, and much of what has been expressed in other ways, using categories variously described as religious, theological or spiritual, about the same behaviour and experience. I believe it is making a category error to oppose what is asserted in two distinct language domains. Moreover, as a Christian, it is my belief that, ultimately, truth is one and that what God has chosen to give to man down the ages through his special messengers will not ultimately conflict with what he has encouraged us to discover as we exercise his gifts of mind and hand in exploring the created order, including, of course, man himself, his experience and his behaviour. That is not to say that there will not be a steady stream of apparent conflicts between what, at any time, we believe to be the case from psychological research, and what we have hitherto understood the Bible to be saying. As we shall see, such conflicts will arise at times because our psychological knowledge is partial or inaccurate, and at times because we have wrongly interpreted Scripture. Either way, unreal conflicts are readily generated. Later parts of this book will illustrate this. Time and again we shall discover how easy it is to assert that particular aspects of religious behaviour can be explained as nothing but the natural outworking of known psychological processes. Equally we shall see how easy it is to give the impression that to attribute change in behaviour to the work of the Holy Spirit is to deny the possibility of understanding the psychological process at work as that change takes place. To take either stand, we shall argue, is misguided and is to commit the error of 'nothing-buttery'. What we mean by this will be explained in detail in the next chapter.

We all like to have a nice tidy comprehensive system into which we can fit what we know, and as psychologists we are no exception. So often however the only honest thing to do is to leave tantalizing loose ends hanging rather than to foreclose an issue when the evidence we have at present is really insufficient to justify our doing so. Equally, as Christians, we are not always as ready as we should be to keep an open mind on matters, such as some of the ones discussed in this book, in which what God is teaching us from our scientific endeavours may suggest some re-thinking of interpretations we have hitherto given to Scripture. It is not that Scripture is in error, but rather our interpretation of it.

The structure of the book will be as follows. Chapter 2 gives a brief account for the non-specialist reader of what psychologists do and what sort of theories they construct in order to make sense of their research data.

In chapter 3 we shall look at what psychologists say about the nature of man, and in so doing we shall outline the main features of the psychological models of man which are most widely favoured by psychologists today. This will put us in a better position to evaluate the meaning of psychological statements and to see how they relate to other statements about behaviour.

Chapter 4 examines the main features of the biblical model of man. Chapter 5 attempts to answer the question of how the biblical and psychological models of man are related. Chapters 6 and 7 arise from comparing the behaviour of men with that of animals and machines. We shall look at the problem of determinism; the use of techniques of behaviour control and behaviour therapy; the implications of increasing knowledge of the biological bases of behaviour; how inherited characteristics and environmental factors influence man's behaviour; questions of individual freedom and responsibility. Chapter 8 compares accounts of religious conversion traditionally given by Christians with some of the accounts offered by psychologists. Chapter 9 looks at other problems which arise because of the overlapping interests of psychologists and Christians. These problems concern guilt, moral awareness and sin.

In chapter 10 we examine psychological theories claiming to account for why men believe in God – theories, for example, that such beliefs are comforting illusions, responses to frustration, reinforcers of acceptable behaviour and extinguishers of unacceptable behaviour. In the final chapter we suggest lines for future thinking, which, if pursued, may throw new light on problems of mutual concern to some psychologists and theologians.

2 Psychology today: its scope, methods and models

At least some of the problems we meet as we try to relate psychology and Christian beliefs arise because of misunderstandings of psychology. For this reason it will be helpful if, before we tackle our main questions, we try to answer some logically prior ones, such as, What is psychology all about? What do psychologists do? What sort of theories do psychologists construct? Are they like any other scientific theories? If not, in what ways do they differ?

Psychology students will certainly not need any convincing about the necessity for this. They will remember all too well their bewilderment after studying psychology for a term at university or college. The variety of subject-matter covered, the methods of investigation described, and the theories proposed all seemed to contribute to a very untidy and heterogeneous subject. Those who teach the subject quite understand this confusion; but in some ways they feel it is a necessary stage to go through. At least it helps to counteract the dogmatic presentations of over-simplified versions of psychology regrettably found so often in the press today. But if those with the opportunity to study psychology as a university discipline can so readily misunderstand its nature and scope, how much more difficult it is for the interested Christian layman who must look mainly to the popular press to tell him about contemporary psychology. No wonder he feels at times that this or that psychological theory is challenging some of his basic beliefs. It is for this reason that in the next few pages we must attempt a thumb-nail sketch of the nature, scope, methods and theories of contemporary psychology. Those who wish to fill out this sketch with more detail are invited to read one or more of the introductory texts listed in the footnote below.[1]

Gaining perspective

In one sense psychology is as old as man. As he has reflected upon his own thoughts and behaviour he has tried to make sense of what he has found there. Equally he has tried to understand why his fellow men behave in this way and not that. Sages, mystics, philosophers and reflective men in all ages have thus, in a real sense, been psychologists. Problems arose, however, when one man's introspections and observations did not agree with another's, when one man's view of what makes a man do this and not that disagreed with his neighbour's view. What then was to be done? Certainly careful analysis, debate and argument could resolve some of the problems; but others remained.

Some groups such as philosophers, theologians and medical practitioners had in the past their own special reasons for understanding man and his behaviour in more detail. Regrettably, their answers were at times so far wide of what we now believe to be the case that we look back with horror at some of the things they did in the name of truth – such things as burning as witches those whom today we would often recognize as mentally ill and in need of care and treatment.

It was not, however, until the last century that we saw the beginning of a psychology based more upon fact than opinion. Psychologists studying sensation began to examine systematically how what is felt is related to the intensity of the stimulus applied. They noted, for example, how the increase in the physical intensity of a light is related to how bright the light appears. They investigated other senses such as touch and hearing in the same way. At the same time other biologists, strongly influenced by Darwin, studied how men and animals express their emotions. Some, often

---

[1] Wright, D. S. *et al.*, *Introducing Psychology: An Experimental Approach* (Penguin, London, 1970). Jeeves, M. A., *Experimental Psychology: An Introduction for Biologists* (Edward Arnold, London, 1974). Miller, G. A., *Psychology: The Science of Mental Life* (Hutchinson, London, 1964). Munn, N. L., *Psychology: The Fundamentals of Human Adjustment*, 6th ed. (Houghton Mifflin, New York, 1972).

expert at observing animals in their natural surroundings, studied how animals solved problems and learned simple tasks. They noticed how learning ability seemed to be systematically related to how complex a nervous system an animal possessed. Renewed interest in mental illness led to more sustained attempts to classify the different types systematically and to look for roots common to the illnesses in any one class.

By the turn of the century we find William James, a physiologist, physician and philosopher, all rolled into one, writing his *Principles of Psychology* – a work we can still read with advantage. He was also a deeply religious man and brought his psychological insights to the task of understanding the amazing variety of religious experiences reported by different people, including his own personal experiences. Shortly before this, in 1879, the first psychological laboratory was established in Leipzig by Wilhelm Wundt. Soon afterwards others were established and those who worked in them thought it perfectly proper to study not only sensation, but also a variety of mental processes variously referred to as 'judgments', 'thoughts' and such like. A great deal of this work, however, failed to produce very much agreement amongst different observers working in different laboratories in different parts of the world.

Soon a strong reaction (led by John B. Watson) developed in America, against so-called introspectionist psychology. He argued that you cannot begin to build a scientific psychology based upon private, subjective data gained from introspection. Behind his stand that psychology should be a science of behaviour was Watson's genuine desire to gain for psychology the obvious advantages of the objective approaches of the physicists and biologists. In the case of psychology, this meant restricting one's observations to overt responses, to the stimuli that produced them and to any observable aspects of underlying physiological mechanisms such as nerves, muscles and glands. In developing his point of view he was influenced by the pioneering work of the Russian physiologist Pavlov on conditioned reflexes. Watson saw Pavlov's techniques as one way of circumventing introspective reports.

There is no doubt that, whilst Watson's approach was not new and its roots can be traced in the history of psychology and biology, it was his particular formulation of the need for an objective psychology, and of one way of achieving it, that set the pattern, since continued in modern psychology, of a preoccupation with behaviour. Along with this has been the development of methods of study as objective as many used in other natural and physical sciences.

We may take advantage of this brief mention of behaviourism to distinguish between behaviourism as a methodology in psychology and the materialistic philosophy which Watson and some behaviourists, since his day, have personally expressed. It is strange in a way that Watson, whilst arguing that psychologists must stick to the facts revealed in their observations and experiments, nevertheless went considerably beyond the facts himself. Many psychologists both then and now, who accept that psychology stands its best chance of systematic development when it is regarded as the natural science of behaviour, flatly reject as philosophically naïve the view that they are thereby forced into accepting a materialistic philosophy. This point is well expressed in what is still probably the most widely used university textbook of psychology. Professor Norman Munn in his chapter on 'Systems in Psychology' has written:

'The present-day psychologist with behaviouristic leanings, who is known merely as a psychologist, might embrace any philosophical or religious viewpoint. This is because behaviouristic psychology is for him a methodology, a means of discovering information about behaviour and in no sense a concept of the nature of ultimate reality. For practical purposes in carrying on his investigations, any scientist must treat what is before him as if it were material, but he has no more notion than anyone else as to what, if anything, lies beyond the range of his senses, even when these are amplified by such instruments of science as microscopes, galvanometers, and electronic devices. As a scientist he can neither affirm nor deny any particular theory or doctrine of ultimate reality. Nor should he be expected to do so, any more than a physicist, a chemist, or a physiologist. Objective psychologists, like individuals in other sciences, actually vary a great deal from one to the other with respect to their philosophical or religious beliefs.'[2]

We shall return to this point later in our own discussions of how those who are psychologists and Christians interpret their total knowledge and experience.

We may note at this stage, however, that to be a behaviourist today does *not* mean that one thereby embraces whole-heartedly Watson's brand of behaviourism. To label a psychologist as a behaviourist today indicates that in his research he emphasizes the study and analysis of behaviour and places little reliance on hypothetical, unobservable mental processes in formulating his explanations of his observations. Certainly to be a behaviourist is not necessarily to be anti-Christian. There are Christian behaviourists and non-Christian anti-behaviourists.

At the same time that Watson was propagating his brand of behaviourism Freud was capturing the imagination, and often the allegiance, of psychologists and psychiatrists on both sides of the Atlantic. Trained as a physician and developing an early specialist interest in neurology, he soon became fascinated by the phenomenon of hypnosis, especially with its application to the treatment of hysterical behaviour. He studied under the famous French neurologist, Charcot, who believed that hysterics alone could be hypnotized. But soon Freud developed his own views that hypnosis as a method could give access to events, desires and fears, unrecognized by his patients in their normal waking lives. Through treating a small number of patients with neurotic illnesses, he soon became convinced of the powerful influence on our behaviour of factors of which we are not normally conscious. This idea that behaviour is so strongly influenced by events of which we are not conscious was revolutionary.

Freud introduced a new form of psychotherapy known as 'psychoanalysis' which made no use of hypnosis. It concentrated

[2] Munn, N. L., *Psychology: The Fundamentals of Human Adjustment*, 6th ed. (Houghton Mifflin, New York, 1972), p. 31.

instead on the use of 'free association', a technique which encouraged patients to talk freely about everything that came to mind as they relaxed on a couch. In particular they were asked to report as fully as possible anything they had dreamt.

From detailed studies of the dreams of his patients Freud became convinced that an understanding of the part played by such unconscious forces was important not only for the understanding of abnormal behaviour but also of everyday life. It was not long before he saw the relevance of his new theories to many aspects of man's life and history, to the arts, to culture, to religion. It was a brave man, indeed, who at that time would call into question the fashionable new psychology, seemingly able to provide a fresh understanding of so many perennial human problems. Of particular popular interest was Freud's conclusion that neurotic disorders result from frustrated sexual desire or from anxiety associated with sex. He believed that early childhood training teaches us not to talk or think about sex and we therefore try to put such ideas out of mind, or as he put it, 'repress' them.

Many psychologists now believe that Freud over-emphasized the influence of sex in human life. Some of his fellow psychoanalysts soon differed from Freud in this regard. Today a more sober assessment of Freud's views has emerged. Few academic psychologists find his views totally convincing or scientifically sound. Some of his most outspoken critics like Eysenck in Britain, and Mowrer in America, have gone so far as to contend that in general he was wrong in his views. Others, taking a slightly less extreme view, would still credit him with at least pointing out the importance of factors of which we are not consciously aware in determining behaviour, especially where these unconscious factors are associated with events that occurred in early childhood.

Whilst psychoanalysis held the public, and often the academic eye, there were other psychologists with more modest aims and more circumscribed objectives working away quietly in new and steadily growing departments of psychology in universities, especially in North America. The period from 1939 to 1945 saw a concentration on applied problems which arose in the war – problems such as how to select the most suitable men and women for the different branches of the armed services, how to design weapons and machinery to match man's capabilities, how to cope with the casualties of war, the brain-injured, the shell-shocked. It was the attempt to help the large number of psychiatric casualties of war which was to present a challenge to the psychoanalytic method of psychotherapy which it could not meet and which found it wanting as a method of treatment capable of dealing with large numbers of patients.

In the post-war era psychology has continued to expand and to flourish. By 1950 Professor Boring of Harvard could point out that, if the rate of increase in the number of psychologists in the USA which had occurred in the first half of the twentieth century was sustained into the second half, then by the year 2000 every other person would be a psychologist! With this explosive increase has come the development of more and more specialist branches within psychology. Some of the specializations are so different from others that members of the different branches at times find it difficult to communicate with each other. Thus a psychologist studying the biochemical bases of behaviour has very little in common with one studying how people behave in small groups. At the same time they both recognize and value the contribution that the other makes to the common task of tackling the almost unbelievably complex problems of understanding behaviour. We shall return to this point later as we consider how to relate the accounts that each gives from his own viewpoint. To ignore the diversity of subject-matter in contemporary psychology, and to fail to recognize the range of concepts employed in building theories to account for the empirical observations in the different branches of the subject, is to ensure that many muddles will be produced, leading to pseudo-conflicts. If there is a place for semantic hygiene anywhere in science today it is certainly in this area.

The object of this brief backward glance has been to help the non-specialist to appreciate how diverse a subject psychology is, how it has taken, and will take, many years to sift out opinion from fact, and how attempts to discredit Christianity, which begin with the bold assertion that 'Psychology says ... ', are more likely to signal a superficial acquaintance with psychology on the part of the speaker than the start of a considered critique of the Christian faith!

Contemporary psychology's scientific aspirations

Most people today agree that there is a measure of objectivity about scientific knowledge which differentiates it from what is variously called common sense, popular opinion or everyday knowledge. That is not to ignore or deny the personal involvement of the scientist in acquiring scientific knowledge – a point developed convincingly by Michael Polanyi.[3] For our limited purposes here, however, we wish to indicate how the application of the so-called scientific method has played an important part in the development of psychology over the past fifty years. The empiricist approach emphasizes the vital importance of careful observation, of a sustained attempt at detecting the regularities in the events of the world around us. Once such regularities are noticed there may follow a hunch about why one event follows another with such consistency. Such a hunch may be dignified with the label of a hypothesis. Deductions are then made from it and you are already involved in applying the so-called hypothetico-deductive method. Further observations are made, either under naturally occurring conditions or in laboratory contrived situations. If the latter is the case, you do your experiment, note the outcome and then either accept your hypothesis with an increased degree of confidence, or refine it, extend it or reject it.

Science thus moves forward by the recurrent application of this process of observation, hypothesis formulation and testing, modification, further observation, experimentation and so on. As the range of applicability of a hypothesis is extended it may be accorded the label of a law. These are sometimes expressed in mathematical terms and, like hypotheses, are subject to modification or rejection as new data are gathered.

It is this scientific method, developed, applied and refined over the last four centuries which has produced the achievements of science which surround us today. When applied to the problems

[3] Polanyi, M., *Personal Knowledge* (Routledge and Kegan Paul, London, 1958).

we confront when we try to understand behaviour it has met with more than limited success and justifies a cautious optimism for the future. As we discover systematic relationships between such sequences of behaviour we produce theories which may or may not make reference to what are usually called mental processes. In tackling some of their problems psychologists believe that much is to be gained from studies of animal behaviour where we can exert greater control of experimental variables including genetic factors.

There are, of course, other areas where no such rigorous control is possible and here we have to rely on data which is difficult to interpret reliably. For example, surveys, using questionnaires, may show that certain things correlate highly with certain other things. But a high correlation does not in itself establish a causal relationship. That may later be established by more controlled laboratory experiments.

Psychology's special problems
Because of the nature of its subject-matter psychology faces special problems in its search for objectivity. Since none of us can simultaneously hold in mind a large catalogue of facts we all make generalizations to help organize and summarize our collected facts or experience. When this is done systematically we may refer to the end product as a theory. We all know how difficult it is to make unbiased judgments and how we are so influenced by our particular upbringing, experience and environment that objective judgments become very difficult. Our private 'psychological theories' about other people illustrate this well. We all tend to select those experiences which fit with our hunches and ignore those which do not. In this way we can retain generalizations hallowed by time but which are not necessarily scientifically supportable. How often, for example, have we heard that 'fat people are good-humoured', that 'people with high foreheads are highly intelligent', that 'a protruding chin goes with guts and determination'. It is because the psychologist is so aware of such difficulties that he has developed various systematic methods for studying behaviour all aimed at reducing to a minimum the

influence of such factors. He knows how an investigator's hopes and fears about the outcome of a study can influence his findings and thus he welcomes the efforts of other psychologists working in different laboratories in other parts of the world to repeat his findings. If they obtain the same results he can feel more confident about his own findings. Where data gathering involves any kind of interviewing, as in psychoanalysis, the effects of personal bias and selective perceiving and remembering are increased enormously and the chances of objectivity recede markedly.

Theories in psychology

Psychologists, like other scientists, are not satisfied simply to discover empirical relationships between events. They also construct theories which contain generalizations from which deductions may be made and applied to many different situations. Psychologists, like other scientists, use concepts which by their nature are not directly observable but help to make sense of the observable events. Such concepts, at times referred to as 'theoretical constructs', do not differ fundamentally from those used in physiology or in physics. The physiologist talks about the sodium pump, the physicist about atoms, protons, neutrons and so on. The psychologist's theoretical constructs, however, tend to apply to a more restricted range of phenomena than those of the physicist.

Sometimes theoretical constructs are clarified by reference to models, usually thought models, but occasionally mechanical or electronic models. Just as physiologists refer to the sodium pump to explain how nervous transmission occurs, so psychologists refer to filters that operate as we selectively attend to some things rather than others occurring in our environment.

There are several different kinds of theory to be found in psychology today. Some, following the process of data gathering and inductive reasoning referred to above and taking the form of concise summaries, become very wide ranging; others are of more restricted application. Some are what might be called the 'what if' kind. Someone says, 'What if the mechanism underlying that kind of behaviour is analogous to this or that model?', often borrowing the model from another science. The best-known contemporary example of this is when we say, 'What if the human brain works in some ways like a computer?' Other examples are Broadbent's filter theory of selective attention or Tinbergen's hydraulic model of instinctive behaviour. Theories in psychology, then, as in other sciences, serve two principal functions. They help to make sense of data gathered from observation and experiment, to summarize it and to integrate it with existing data. They also help to suggest and to guide further lines of research.

Psychologists do not claim to have a monopoly of understanding people. They certainly do not claim to have any exclusive rights to notions of why people act, as we say, 'in character', of why they act predictably in certain situations. The world's great literature contains many profound insights into what guides, motivates and orders human behaviour. Wise men deeply involved in practical affairs become very shrewd judges of the behaviour of their fellow men. Where psychology differs from these is that it tries to move from intuitive, largely private, hunches to the formulation of testable hypotheses, formulated as rigorously as possible. It seeks to move from the description or explanation of behaviour in everyday terms towards the formulation of explanations using terms defined as precisely as possible. Such terms are said to be 'operationally defined' and refer explicitly to events observable by anyone with the appropriate training assisted, where necessary, by specially developed instruments. Moreover, the psychologist seeks to make his observations no longer under everyday conditions where so many random occurrences make the isolation of causal sequences extremely difficult, but under conditions of his own devising with as much control over unwanted extraneous events as possible. In the next chapter we shall look in a little more detail at examples of four different kinds of theory currently influential in psychology. Before we do so, however, let us look briefly at what we mean when we say that we explain someone's behaviour psychologically.

Explanation in psychology
When it comes to deciding what kind of explanation or what level

of explanation is most appropriate for any set of observational data one finds that different psychologists hold different views based not solely on scientific data, but on their personal values, philosophies and hopes. Some, today a minority, believe that the goal of all explaining is ultimately to reduce everything to the most fundamental level possible such as the sub-atomic. Others take the view that the level of explanation invoked must be appropriate to, and do justice to, the complexity of the behaviour being studied. We must consider this now in a little more detail since it is an issue recurring frequently in our subsequent discussions of how we relate psychological and religious explanations of behaviour.

Like other sciences, psychology as it has developed has produced areas of specialization. These usually arise through focusing attention on specific problems. In tackling these problems special techniques of investigation are needed which are often borrowed or adapted from related natural sciences. Despite the range of topics covered today by psychologists, a little probing nevertheless confirms that what we have just written about the application of the scientific method is substantially true of these diverse branches. Since each specialization, however, not only develops its own techniques but also its own vocabulary, the question is sometimes asked, 'How does the account of this or that aspect of behaviour given by a specialist in one branch of psychology relate to the account given in a different jargon by one of his colleagues specializing in another branch?' Let us illustrate this and then ask how we see these different accounts in relation to one another.

One of the central concerns of psychologists (some would say *the* central problem) is how learning takes place. We want to know what factors facilitate learning, what factors interfere with it and so on. One approach to this problem which has had a great deal of research effort devoted to it in the last twenty years concentrates on studying how the amount of reward (or punishment) which produces a correct response (or error), and the timing of the giving of the reward, are systematically related to the rate of learning.

The pioneer here is Professor B. F. Skinner, whose particular jargon refers to contingencies of reinforcement, or more colloquially as he himself once put it,

> 'What all this and that complicated verbiage means is we are studying the ways in which the consequences of behaviour are contingent upon what an organism is doing in a given situation.'[4]

This is an approach which can be effectively used to study some forms of both human and animal learning. The particular technique developed by Skinner was especially appropriate for studying learning in rats or pigeons. It consisted of a small box in one end of which there was a lever and below the lever a small dish-like container where food pellets could be dropped. When the animal pressed the lever he could receive a food pellet. How much food he received and how often would depend upon the schedule of reinforcement under which he was working. On some schedules of reinforcement the rat would be rewarded for every lever press; on others only after so many presses; on others only after so much time had elapsed since the last reward. Under other conditions the rat could press the lever to end an electric shock through the grid he stood on, and soon he would learn that by pressing the lever at the appropriate time he could avoid the shock altogether. These and other variations will be familiar to psychology students, as will the 'Skinner Box'.

Another psychologist might use the same piece of apparatus but be interested in discovering which parts of the brain are especially important for the establishment of certain kinds of learning. Unlike his colleague who was using the technique as a means of answering the question of what factors influence rate of learning in terms of schedules of reinforcement, this other man will be interested in learning something about how the structure and function of the nervous system affects rate of learning. Yet another colleague, also in the same laboratory, may be interested in how the chemical composition of the body, and especially of

---

[4] From *Firing Line*, a transcript of a TV programme dated 17 October 1971, p. 6.

the brain and related structures, changes in the course of learning or how the course of learning can be influenced by the use of drugs.

With little modification an apparatus similar to a Skinner Box can be used to study how learning is facilitated by the presence of other animals and of how they may co-operate in a learning situation. This approach may be developed even further to study how small-group learning in animals is influenced by the size and make-up of the group. Or, yet again, another colleague interested in individual differences may be selectively breeding different kinds of animals so that after many generations he produces what are known as 'maze-bright' and 'maze-dull' animals.

Now the reason we have gone into so much detail over this point is that from their different standpoints all these psychologists, often working in the same laboratory, studying the same behaviour, and tackling the same general problem, namely, What factors affect rate of learning?, will formulate their answers in different terms. One will refer to schedules of reinforcement, one to cerebral organization, one to the enzyme systems controlling the biochemical constitution of the brain, one to behaviour in pairs, one to behaviour in small groups and another to genetic loadings. Are these different explanations to be regarded as competitors? Do these investigators have to parcel out carefully the topics they are studying so that there is no overlap in their interests? Does the one interested in schedules of reinforcement face the prospect ultimately of becoming redundant as his physiologically orientated colleagues reduce the problem to one of synapses? Or does the physiological psychologist see his eventual demise as the biochemist makes him redundant, reducing everything to biochemistry? Or come to that, are they all only in business until the physicist shows why, at the end of the day, everything can be reduced to an explanation at the level of sub-atomic particles? The answer to all these questions is 'No'. Whilst each believes that, given enough time (another 2,000 years or so!) and resources, he can come up with an exhaustive account in his jargon, at his level, that will not thereby establish that his account is the exclusive one to which all others must give way.

The problem of how properly to relate these different explanations arises in two distinct ways for psychologists. First, as we have just indicated by reference to the variety of explanations which can be given of learning, it arises within psychology itself as one attempts to build an integrated picture from the efforts of specialist groups within psychology. Second, it arises because of psychology's position spanning the biological sciences and the social sciences. By virtue of its intermediate position psychology finds itself involved in a two-way interaction – on the one hand between psychology and physiology, and on the other between social studies and psychology. Physiology looks to psychology to formulate explanations in terms of functional units larger than, for example, the cell or the synapse. This is the opposite of the reductionist approach. With the social sciences, psychology 'provides a means of conceptualizing the detailed mechanisms of the behaviour of groups and organized social units'.[5] At the same time psychologists like Argyle insist that most of the essential human characteristics cannot be manifested by a person in isolation. Argyle's approach to the understandings of social interaction illustrates rather well the importance of taking account of other levels of explanation within psychology – on what we might call the horizontal plane – as well as other levels of explanation above and below on the vertical plane. The vertical plane, in this context, refers to research in anthropology and linguistics (above) as well as ethology and animal behaviour (below). The latter, for example, draws attention to the evolutionary and instinctive roots of social behaviour, the sensory channels and methods of signalling used, and the biological and other drives which produce social interaction.

This immediately introduces the notion of a hierarchy of explanations in which, for example, psychology would appear below anthropology but above physiology. To attempt to expand the terms of reference of physiology so as to embrace psychology is as much to expand physiology as to reduce psychology – a point not always apparent in the writings of some reductionists. Whether science is to be unified by proceeding

[5] Welford, A. T., *Fundamentals of Skill* (Methuen, London, 1968), p. 335.

upwards or downwards through this hypothetical hierarchy is still an open question. But to return to psychology. Most psychologists agree with the tacit assumption that their primary concern is with the behaviour of the whole organism. This is not to deny the importance and relevance of levels of explanation which are given by those who concentrate on the behaviour of the individual in a social context, or upon the study of mechanisms and processes going on within organisms which gives rise to levels of explanation of what may be called an intra-organismic kind. *All* are necessary to begin to do full justice to the complexity of man's behaviour.

Granted, however, that there are no logical or empirical grounds for any one level of explanation laying claim to being the only valid level, two questions remain. Are there then no limits to the number of explanations we must accept? Second, are there any criteria for helping us decide whether two explanations are complementary or competing? We may reformulate these two questions as one more general question as follows: If the different explanations offered by psychologists to the same set of events (our horizontal plane) as well as those offered at other levels by sociologists or physiologists (our vertical plane) are not to be regarded as competitors, then how are they to be related? As has often been pointed out the clue to our problem may be found within science itself. It was a solution arrived at fifty years ago by physicists studying the nature of light.

A hundred years ago the orthodox way of picturing light was in terms of waves spreading through space. The evidence for this view was very convincing and it seemed clear that the earlier view of picturing light as a stream of particles was wrong and could be better done without. But then only fifty years ago the situation changed again when it was discovered that, in certain previously unexplored situations, light seemed to behave quite definitely like a hail of tiny particles. Now the question was, Which is the valid picture, the wave or the particle one? Only after a lot of hard thinking did it become clear that the correct answer was that both pictures could be valid. In fact the two pictures were not rivals, but complementary. Furthermore it became clear that you could never deduce contradictory conclusions by a valid use of both because they represented answers to different kinds of questions. Ultimately it is only the facts of experience that can convince us that both accounts are necessary. We are here dealing with a logical, not a scientific, point, but it is one which, it seems, is open to very ready abuse and misunderstanding and for this reason we must seek to see clearly the conditions under which it can legitimately be used.

One attempt to specify under what conditions two or more descriptions may legitimately be regarded as logically complementary is found in a paper by D. M. MacKay.[6] The conditions he sets out may be summarized as follows: (1) that they purport to have a common reference; (2) that each is in principle exhaustive (in the sense that none of the entities or events comprising the common reference need be left unaccounted for); yet (3) they make different assertions because (4) the logical preconditions of definition and/or of the use (that is the context in which they are set) of concepts or relationships in each are mutually exclusive, so that the significant aspects referred to in one are necessarily omitted from the other. MacKay also points out that 'nothing in the idea of logical complementarity excludes the possibility of a higher mode of representation which could synthesize two or more complementary descriptions; nor is it necessary that one description should be inferrable from the other. The label is useful mainly as a warning not to try to relate such descriptions in the wrong way, by treating them as (a) referring to different things, (b) synonymous, (c) inexhaustive, or (d) contradictory.'

The somewhat negative, yet nonetheless important, point which emerges here is that, before explanations at different levels in different jargon are debated as rivals, it is obligatory that we should establish that they are not, in fact, complementary. What applies to the relation of these different scientific explanations applies also to the task of relating religious and scientific accounts of behaviour. In both cases it is essential to realize that proof of complementarity does not establish that either account is true.

[6] MacKay, D. M., *Aristotelian Society Supplement*, 1958, Vol. 32, pp. 105-122.

Uses and abuses of models in psychology

In the past, failure to grasp the complementary nature of different explanations of behaviour has at times produced pseudo-conflicts. As more and more data have accumulated from research effort guided by one or other of the particular approaches to the study of behaviour outlined earlier, it has become possible to formulate thought models which act as powerful conceptual tools to guide further research and to apply tentatively to new situations. Such models are of the kind described earlier as performing a 'what if' function. For example, we may say, 'what if' the human operator, in picking up information from his surroundings and acting upon it, functions in some respects like a complex, very high speed computer? What follows from this? Or 'what if' the behaviour of men has striking counterparts in some respects to the behaviour of some sub-human organisms? What useful predictions and deductions about his behaviour can we make from this model? What clues, for example, might this give to the control of aggressive behaviour in humans? Or again, 'what if', following Skinner's approach, man functions in some situations like a stimulus-response machine whose behaviour is shaped and maintained by contingencies of reinforcement? Are there clues here which, in addition to making us better circus trainers, may also help to train children or modify abnormal behaviour? Let us examine a little more closely some of these models and the 'what ifs' that seem to flow from them.

Students of the physical, chemical or biological sciences are familiar with models which assume or imply a mechanistic explanation, either of a particular aspect of man's biological functioning, or of man as a whole. There is, of course, nothing new in giving such mechanistic explanations. Earlier generations of biologists used similar though less sophisticated models, for example of the heart as a pump. The main difference today is the degree of precision and sophistication achieved in model and theory building, especially in subjects such as biochemistry and biophysics.

Conscious of the determinist flavour of many such mechanistic explanations, it is not surprising that a student begins to wonder whether, after all, man is nothing but an extremely complex machine. He will recognize, of course, that there are, so to speak, machines within machines, possibly organized in a hierarchy, but the general impression that develops is that it is a mechanistic view that makes most sense of our knowledge and understanding of man today.

Perhaps the outstanding example of this, and certainly, as we shall see later, the one most relevant to a rethinking of our traditional views of man, arises from what we know about how the central nervous system works. Both behavioural and biological scientists are familiar with models of how information is picked up, transduced, transmitted, processed and reacted to, and of the part played by the central nervous system in all this.

It is then but a short step to the view that even the most complicated forms of behaviour should ultimately, and in principle, be capable of description in mechanistic terms of a similar kind. Add to this the accumulating evidence about the intimate relationship between nervous system functioning and behaviour, and the resultant picture is one which suggests that man's behaviour, both simple and complex, will eventually be explicable in mechanistic terms. The problem then becomes, Is man then nothing but a complex machine?

Another 'what if' problem arises from courses in the behavioural sciences dealing with comparative psychology and the biological bases of behaviour. Students taking such courses often become concerned when they discover how many of the psychological processes studied in man can be profitably investigated through studying animals.

The impression sometimes given by such courses is that basic psychological processes studied in man, whether perceiving, learning, remembering, or problem-solving, as well as his emotional responses and instinctive behaviour, can be fully and adequately studied by investigating either non-human primates or, in some instances, animals considerably lower in the phylo-genetic scale. In the light of such accumulating evidence the question naturally arises, Is man then nothing but an unusually complex and highly developed animal?

'What if' problems are not confined to the physical and biological sciences. Students of sociology and anthropology learn about the formative influence of the social and cultural environments upon attitudes, beliefs and behaviour, and they can easily gain the impression that man is nothing but the resultant of fortuitous environmental circumstances. In a wider context this means that a man is what he is because of the formative influence of his cultural environment (part of the subject-matter of social anthropology), and in the narrower context that he is moulded by the effects of living in smaller groupings such as family and school.

We see, then, how 'what if' approaches can lead to a variety of forms of 'nothing-buttery', whether it is that man is nothing but a complex machine, or nothing but a particularly highly developed animal, or nothing but the product of environmental forces. From a Christian point of view, nothing whatever is to be gained by seeking to deny that, as part of the tactics of scientific research, much is to be gained by developing and testing models of man as a complex machine, by recognizing how important clues to brain and behaviour relations in man can be found from studies on animals, and that to some extent man shares features of his behaviour repertoire with animals, and that, within limits, a man's behaviour is heavily dependent upon the circumstances in which he has developed. What we must look at carefully is the implication that such procedural and research benefits necessarily lead to the conclusion that man is therefore nothing but each of the things we listed.

What we wrote earlier about how to relate different kinds of explanation will have exposed the logical mistake committed by each of the kinds of nothing-buttery just described.

We have argued that it is mistaken, both on logical grounds and on empirical grounds, to assert that psychology can be reduced without remainder to physiology. Logically it is tantamount to saying that a 'fasten your seat belts' sign is nothing but wires and bulbs, and therefore you may ignore it, or that the words addressed to you by a friend are nothing but sounds analysable without remainder on a sound spectrograph. Empirically it is evident that there are questions – questions, for example, about interpersonal relations – which cannot even be properly formulated let alone answered if reference is made only to physiological mechanisms. The choice of one approach which, in itself, may be extremely productive and lead to important discoveries can at the same time preclude even the formulation of equally important questions about the same events but at a different level.

This, then, is a simple but basic point, and failure to grasp it is at the root of a good deal of meaningless and fruitless debate today. To assert, as we are doing here, that at times it may be necessary, in order to do justice to the complexity of the phenomenon we are studying, to tackle it from several different standpoints, at different conceptual levels, is not, as we have also seen, to say that any explanation goes, however way-out and fanciful. Each must show that that kind of explanation is necessary to do justice to the totality of what is being studied and each must bring forward the evidence relevant to the level which is being advocated. We shall return to this matter of complementary descriptions from time to time as we discuss specific issues where psychological explanations have been presented as competitors with religious explanations of behaviour.

3 Evaluating contemporary theories

Contemporary psychology is a mass of facts and a mass of theories. The Einstein of psychology has not yet appeared. There is no simple unifying theory which is generally accepted by all psychologists. The reasons for this are not hard to find. With a subject-matter covering the behaviour of organisms from molluscs to mice and to men, it would be surprising, indeed, if all the data could be handled with the same theoretical constructs.

In this chapter we shall try to give the non-psychologist a feel of what contemporary psychological theories are like and what they do. Those selected are either the ones supposed to be most in conflict with Christian beliefs (psychoanalysis and ethology, for example) or those most generally used by psychologists who regard their subject as a natural or behavioural science.

The majority of psychologists believe that it is early days yet to be looking for anything approaching a comprehensive model. At this stage in the development of psychology, they say, we should be content with constructing models which can cope with the data from particular specialist areas within psychology. By looking at some of these models in more detail we shall better understand why it is mistaken to regard them as competitors with models of man and his nature which occur in religious and other non-scientific literature. Four will be described. I have chosen them to give some idea of the wide spectrum of views found in psychology today. The first will be the Freudian psychoanalytic model. One reason for selecting this is that, for many people, psychology is still synonymous with psychoanalysis. Moreover, in some non-professional circles it is firmly believed that traditional Freudian theory is well founded and generally accepted by all psychologists. Associated with this view one often finds a ready acceptance of Freud's conclusion that to believe in a God is to place one's faith in an illusion.

The second model will be familiar to students studying in university departments of psychology, which is one of my reasons for considering it. Another is because it is so different from the Freudian model. It is one of the 'what if' variety mentioned above. Basically it says, 'What if man is regarded as an information gathering and processing system? What follows from this for our wider view of man and his nature?' An additional reason for considering it is that, in some of its more popular versions, it implies that man is 'nothing but' a particularly complex and high speed computer.

The third model is one which over the last few years has been given widespread publicity through the highly speculative and controversial writings of men such as Desmond Morris and, to a lesser extent, Konrad Lorenz. It provides a good example of the kind of model which emerges from the study of animal behaviour and which undoubtedly provides important clues to a deeper understanding of aspects of human behaviour. It is, however, unusually prone to abuse, as, for example, when rather wild and unjustified extrapolations are made from it into areas where its relevance and applicability are questionable, to say the least.

Finally, we shall look at the approach to the study of behaviour associated primarily with the name of Professor B. F. Skinner. The last few years have witnessed considerable controversy over Skinner, not so much on account of his laboratory studies but because of his widely publicized personal philosophy contained in books such as *Beyond Freedom and Dignity*.[1]

Psychoanalytic views of man
In the minds of many people the terms 'psychology' and 'psycho-

[1] Skinner, B. F., *Beyond Freedom and Dignity* (Alfred A. Knopf, New York, 1971; Jonathan Cape, London, 1972).

analysis' have become almost synonymous. Part of the vocabulary of Freudian psychoanalysis has found its way into common usage so that people speak freely of repression, inhibition and the unconscious. Furthermore, the ideas attached to such terms are found to permeate many modern novels and plays. Unfortunately common usage is no guarantee of correct usage and our first task must be, therefore, to give a very truncated account of the main features of the psychoanalytic model epitomized by Freudian theory.

Impressed by the influence of events and memories of which a man is no longer conscious, Freud, early in his theorizing, distinguished between the conscious and the unconscious mind. This was later to be developed as he saw the total personality of a man organized around three major systems. Interaction of these major systems was to be the key to many of his explanations of both normal and abnormal behaviour. What he had previously labelled as the unconscious now came to be known as the 'id'. This was the part of a man which was concerned with the discharge of his basic drives, his energy and his tension. The part of a man's personality previously described as the conscious mind became the 'ego'. This was responsible for regulating his interaction with his environment. To these two systems Freud was to add the 'super-ego', which was that part of a man which encapsulated and represented the moral demands and the judgments of right and wrong which he attempted to hold and to live by.

Since Freud was continually collecting new information about human personality it should be remembered that this gave rise to fairly continuous self-criticism. As a result he constantly revised his theories over a period of almost half a century. It is for this reason that it is difficult to nail down exactly what is meant by psychoanalytic doctrine unless, at the same time, one specifies whether it comes from the early or the late part of Freud's life. The id which supplied the instinctual energy which was driving the personality of a man was seen by Freud as further divisible into two separate groups of instincts. The first group subserve the purposes of life and its continuation and the energy deriving from these he called 'libido'. The second group, never so fully expounded by Freud, were concerned with man's capability for destruction. These were regarded as the source of aggression, sadism and even suicide.

The life instincts were also linked closely with one of Freud's other fundamental notions, his so-called 'pleasure principle'. This asserted that all activities of the mind are driven by the need to reduce or eliminate the tension generated by the id. This tension arises because, whilst the id is trying to operate according to the pleasure principle, the ego must operate according to the reality principle. Operating according to the reality principle means coping with the challenges of the day-to-day world, and devising plans of action acceptable to the occasion. With a little ingenuity, perception, learning, thinking and memory could all be discussed within Freud's model of personality.

As a child grows up the need to respond to the examples and directives of parents, teachers and other adults leads to the development of the third part of the personality, the super-ego. The child tries to tailor his behaviour so that it is approved by his parents. In so doing two separate sub-systems develop within the super-ego. There is the so-called 'ego ideal', which is the model the child holds before him as the one to which he must seek to fit his own behaviour; and there is the 'conscience', which is his summary of what his parents and other adults will disapprove of and condemn as morally bad. According to Freud's views the 'ego ideal' is developed through being rewarded and the conscience through being punished. On this view the super-ego is the repository of a person's social norms.

This is not the place to continue this exposition of Freudian theory and his use of terms like repression, phobias, free-floating anxiety, sublimation, projection, reaction formation, fixation, regression, and so on, many of which are now in our everyday vocabulary. Our task here is to say enough to give the general reader the feel of Freud's notion of personality and the theory which he held. One summary of it which catches its essential flavour rather well is that given by Professor J. S. Bruner. He wrote:

'Freud's is a theory or a proto-theory peopled with actors. The characters are from life; the blind, energetic, pleasure seeking id; priggish and punitive super ego; the ego, battling for its being by diverting the energy of others through its own use. The drama has an economy and a terseness. The ego develops canny mechanisms for dealing with the threat of id impulses; denial, projection, and the rest. Balances are struck between the actors, and in the balance is character and neurosis. Freud was using the dramatic technique of decomposition, the play whose actors are parts of a single life.'[2]

As the theory was developed so Freud began to put forward ideas of the psycho-sexual development of the normal child and, in doing so, he soon drew not only criticism but also ridicule, especially from those who had not looked sympathetically at the evidence which he believed supported his views. Commenting on this and trying to be sympathetic to what Freud has contributed, Miller has written:

'Freud's theories often seem absurd, if not downright false, to readers who encounter them first in a brief summary such as this. It is an easy exercise for a detached outsider to be critical; Freud has little to say to someone who is not personally involved in psychoanalysis. Those who are involved, however, are usually less confident in their criticisms. Once the psychoanalytic expedition back into childhood begins, once the personal commitment to the therapeutic process is given, once one tries to look honestly at oneself, it is no longer so obvious what is reasonable and what is absurd. There is some merit to the claim that the criticism of psychoanalysis is best left to those who have experienced it. In this respect, at least, it is more like a way of life than a scientific theory.'[3]

[2] Bruner, J. S., 'Freud and the Image of Man' in *Partisan Review*, Summer 1956, 23, p. 343, quoted in Miller, G. A., *Psychology: the Science of Mental Life* (Hutchinson, London, 1964).
[3] Miller, G. A., *op. cit.*, p. 244.

Eysenck has taken up this point in developing his own critique of psychoanalysis. He has written:

'It is not often realized to what extent this "emotional biassing" through training analysis forms a complete barrier between analyst and critic. Thus Freud states that "the teachings of psychoanalysis are based upon an incalculable number of observations and experiences, and no one who has not repeated those observations upon himself or upon others is in a position to arrive at an independent judgment of it." Thus Freud demands effectively that one must believe in his system before one can criticize it, a demand which is hardly in line with orthodox scientific procedures! Similar claims are made by the Jungians, where Jacobi states that "theoretic conceptions as explanations are adequate only up to a certain point for the comprehension of Jung's system of thought, for in order to understand it completely one must have experienced its vital working on one's self." When it is realized that there are some fifteen or more hostile "analytic" systems making similar claims, it will be clear that no one can be competent to judge between them because no one would have enough time and money to undergo fifteen separate and incompatible personal training analyses!'[4]

One of the curious things about psychoanalytic theory is that, whilst it has been rejected in general by experts in the field of psychology and other behavioural sciences, it has been readily accepted by the man in the street and by intelligent people in the arts. Since some of the main critics of psychoanalysis have been found amongst professional psychologists and anthropologists, it is important that we should ask ourselves why the man in the street has accepted it so readily. Some have suggested that, because the notions of psychoanalytic theory have a sufficiently close fit with what we might call 'common sense psychology' (the sort of psychology which attempts to give us some sort of understanding of ourselves and our fellow human beings), and therefore meets

[4] Eysenck, H. J., *Uses and Abuses of Psychology* (Pelican, London, 1953), p. 230.

an immediate felt need, it is accordingly readily accepted. Others have pointed out that it is a lazy man's way of explaining, *post hoc*, almost any behaviour one can think of. The view of those psychologists concerned with the development of a scientifically based psychology of the kind outlined in chapter 2 is that, whilst seeking to gain such understanding, at the same time we are equally concerned to generate and to submit to critical test any such explanations of behaviour that are offered. When it comes to giving coherent explanations which will generate precise and testable predictions psychoanalytic theory is found seriously wanting.

It is also important to remember that because psychoanalysts may, at times, be correct in their own surmises, hunches and insights about their fellow men, this does not validate their theories. Such competence is also shown by people who have never heard of psychology or psychoanalysis. We all know of some very astute judges of human motives and behaviour; indeed, the great literature of the world testifies to their existence long before psychoanalysis or scientific psychology appeared on the scene.

What is not sufficiently appreciated is that to be able to offer a possible explanation of some aspect of behaviour does not in itself give any grounds for believing that that explanation is correct or that it is more correct than several others which could also be offered of the same piece of behaviour. This is an important point, particularly when one attempts a serious evaluation of psychoanalytic theory in the light of empirical data which in some circumstances means experimental results.

One of the most recent attempts to evaluate psychoanalytic theory, and one which presents a detailed and scholarly survey of various studies designed to put psychoanalytic theory to experimental test, is contained in a book by Kline entitled *Fact and Fantasy in Freudian Theory*.[5] After examining hundreds of studies he concludes that 'any blanket rejection of Freudian theory as a whole simply flies in the face of the evidence' (p. 346). The care with which Kline carries out his task of critical appraisal makes

[5] Kline, P., *Fact and Fantasy in Freudian Theory* (Methuen, London, 1972).

his conclusion a compelling one even to the professional psychologist who tends to be sceptical of psychoanalytic theory. How
much more convincing, then, to the non-psychologist, particularly if he has a prior disposition to believe and to accept Freudian
theory. A word of caution, however, is required even here. The
complexity of the issues involved and the cleavage in views
amongst professional psychologists is highlighted by Professor
Eysenck's immediate response to Kline's book, first in an article
in the *Bulletin of the British Psychological Society*[6] and secondly by his
own book written in collaboration with Glen Wilson, entitled
The Experimental Study of Freudian Theories.[7] In this most recent
book of Eysenck's we find him taking the papers which Kline
and others regarded as the best evidence in favour of Freudian
theory and claiming that on close examination they all fail to
provide any such proof.

As he put it, after reviewing Kline's book in his paper in the
Bulletin of the British Psychological Society,

'I would conclude . . . that this conscientious scholarly and well-
documented summary of the most convincing evidence for
Freudian theories leaves the reader little option but to conclude
that, if this is the best that can be offered by way of support,
then the only conclusion can be that there is no evidence at all
for psychoanalytic theory.'

Eysenck's views may be somewhat extreme in their criticism.
Nevertheless, there are others, perhaps initially more sympathetic
to psychoanalytic theory, who reach substantially similar conclusions in their evaluation of psychoanalysis as a science. For
example, B. Farrell, in an early paper entitled 'Psychoanalysis –
The Method', concludes after a careful critical appraisal of the
methodology of psychoanalysis that:

---

[6] Eysenck, H. J., 'The Experimental Study of Freudian Concepts' in the *Bulletin
of the British Psychological Society*, 25 (1972), pp. 261–267.
[7] *The Experimental Study of Freudian Theories*, ed. Eysenck, H. J., and Wilson, G. W.
(Methuen, London, 1973).

'It will be difficult to bring analysts satisfactorily within the world of medicine, or the universities, or research institutes and the like, as long as strong suspicions remain that their methods of training resemble techniques of indoctrination rather than those of education. Again, it will probably be many years before this problem is resolved. In the long interim our Society will have to tolerate in its midst a small group of queer and insecure fish, whom the Society cannot comfortably house, and who do not themselves know where they belong.'[8]

Faced with the fact that sustained attempts to derive predictions from psychoanalytic theory and to test them empirically have either proved difficult, or where they have proved possible, have failed to find support for the theory, the psychoanalyst can still fall back on the assertion that, at least as a means of psychotherapy, his system works. Even this, however, is a view which is difficult to defend when the evidence, though so far inconclusive, increasingly points to the fact that, for every two out of three patients who improve during psychotherapy or psychoanalytic methods, two out of three improve without any psychotherapy at all. This is not the place to pursue a detailed review of the literature seeking to evaluate the evidence for Freudian theory. The references given below will provide a useful starting-point for any who wish to do this.

After what has just been written it will doubtless seem odd to conclude that, in spite of everything, we must continue to be grateful to Freud for the way he stirred up the psychological pool at a time when it was becoming stagnant and lifeless. Since it is sometimes asserted that Eysenck's criticisms do not do justice to Freud's contribution, let me quote again from Eysenck. He writes:

'Like most psychologists, I appreciate the breath of fresh air which Freud introduced into the musty dry-as-dust atmosphere of nineteenth century academic psychology. The brilliance of

[8] Farrell, B., 'Psychoanalysis – The Method', reproduced in *Explanation in the Behavioural Sciences*, ed. Borger, R. and Cioffi, F. (CUP, New York, 1970).

his mind has opened doors which no one now would wish to close again, and his keen insight has given us a store-house of theories and hypotheses which will keep researchers busy for many years to come. All this one can appreciate without accepting the totality of his views as revelations from a higher authority, and without losing one's critical sense. There is much that is supremely important in Freud's contribution to psychology, but there is also much that is bad. To eliminate the latter, without losing the former, must be the task of a scientifically-orientated psychology.'[9]

Miller takes up the theme of Freud's contribution when he points out that 'Freud struggled to see man as he is, not as he ought to be or as Freud would have liked to imagine him', and this meant that:

'After he had completed his demonstration of the importance of the unconscious, instinctual forces in human conduct, the old faith in the inevitability of human progress through man's constant growth of knowledge and understanding sounded like an innocent myth concocted to amuse little children.'[1]

Miller's conclusion is that 'Few men have influenced us so deeply'.

Whether Freud's influence advanced or retarded the development of psychology is an issue about which psychologists themselves are sharply divided. The debate no doubt will continue for many years. On the evidence presently available my views can be summed up as follows.

Any attempt to evaluate the contribution that Freud made to the development of psychology must take account of the fact that he worked firmly within the tradition of the nineteenth-century scientists. Like Darwin, his methods were essentially to observe, to classify, to think inductively and to formulate a

[9] Eysenck, H. J., *Uses and Abuses of Psychology* (Pelican, London, 1953).
[1] Miller, G. A., *Psychology: The Science of Mental Life* (Hutchinson, London, 1964), pp. 246 f.

theory which would provide a framework for interpreting his own observations and reinterpreting related existing knowledge. Today, by contrast, we adopt a predominantly experimental approach, coupled with the hypothetico-deductive method. This essential difference in approach has not always been given due weight by some of today's critics of Freud and his later disciples. Neither have they always done justice to Freud when, though rightly criticizing the ineffectiveness of psychoanalytic methods to treat the more serious forms of mental illness – the psychoses – they have failed to remember that Freud himself did not regard such psychotic conditions as treatable by his methods.

Freud has also been criticized on the grounds that he was mistaken to believe that events recalled in the course of psychoanalysis were true and reliable accounts of what really happened. Whilst it is the case that from Freud's early writings it would appear that he believed that such memories of childhood experiences were true, nevertheless from his later writings he evidently seriously questioned their reliability. Indeed, some have claimed that it was a tribute to his genius that he realized that it is just as important to reveal and explore fantasy as fact.

As regards the question of whether Freudian psychotherapy can materially assist in the treatment of neurosis, the Freudian psychologist would, with some justification, insist that his understanding of neurotic illness has changed our whole outlook upon mental illness, in particular, and upon life in general. Whether the change is for the better must remain, however, a matter for serious debate; personally, I doubt it. Neither psychologists in general, nor Christian psychologists in particular, are agreed about this. The view expressed by psychologists like Eysenck that the effectiveness of psychoanalytic therapy remains unproven has been countered by the psychoanalysts' assertion that Eysenck has a mistaken view of how spontaneous remissions come about.

The analysts would maintain that they may occur in several ways, such as (1) cyclic changes in the manifestation of the disease process, (2) subsidence of symptoms without real change in underlying personality stresses, or (3) real improvements in the integration of personality due to maturation and insight following the events of daily life, and to miscellaneous contacts with other people bringing about harmonious changes rather than intensifying difficulties. It is only remissions within the latter group, say the analysts, which are properly comparable with the effects of psychoanalytic therapy. Psychoanalysts could also assert that Freud was not content with symptom removal, otherwise he would never have moved away from his original use of hypnosis. They thus contend that it is not legitimate to compare psychoanalytic therapy with behaviour therapy. Relief from symptoms is important, they agree, but not as important as the reduction of the deep-seated stresses which they claim give rise to the symptoms. Such a posture does seem to me, however, to be advocating a position of special privilege for psychoanalysis, rendering it virtually immune from the normal canons of assessment of scientific theories. As a result, equally competent psychologists remain deeply divided over what to make of psychoanalysis. The issues are complex. But one thing is clear; it is unwise and inadvisable for theologians or anyone else to build a large superstructure upon a foundation so liable to change or rejection as psychoanalytic theory.

Information processing models of man

Whilst the Freudian psychoanalytic model of man is widely known, imprecise, unscientific, and largely rejected by academic psychologists, the one we shall consider next is, by contrast, little known outside professional circles, but is precise, scientific and put to widespread use by academic psychologists. Like so many models in psychology, past and present, it is borrowed from other scientific disciplines. In this case it comes from communication theory and computer science and technology. For those who have gained the impression that psychology inevitably competes and conflicts with Christian faith it may be a helpful exercise if, as we briefly describe this model, they ask themselves at each point with what specific aspect of Christian teaching does this or that aspect of the model conflict.

Being derived from communication theory this model begins with the observation that the organism is sensitive to energy changes in its environment. By energy changes we mean, for example, that there are changes in light impinging on the retina, changes in sounds being picked up by the ear, changes in smells and in the effects of touch; in other words, there are changes in the influx of energy impinging upon an organism through its various sense receptors. These energy changes are transformed by the eye, the ear and so on, into messages which are coded and sent *via* the nervous system to the brain, where they are further processed and dealt with according to certain established routines on the basis of which an appropriate response is made by the organism.

Now this particular model can be used not only as an information flow model in the way that has just been described, but can also be adapted so that fairly precise mathematical relationships can be established between the properties of the stimulus and the properties of the response to that stimulus.

In more recent years, another aspect of communication system theory, known as signal detection theory, has proved extremely valuable to experimental psychologists. This is because it can take account, not only of the nature of the stimuli, but also of the variables within the organism itself, such as readiness to respond depending upon how sure one is that a stimulus has or has not been received. This is not the place to go into detail about either of these approaches. I simply want to make the point that they can be formulated in fairly precise mathematical terms. *This being so, it should become clearer why a moment ago I suggested that, when tempted to put psychological models of man in conflict with Christian doctrine, it may be helpful to ask in what way does this or that mathematical equation, which is one way of expressing this particular psychological model of man, conflict with what the Bible has to say about man?* When the question is put in this way it is difficult to see the grounds for the supposed conflict. A reader may justly complain, however, that he was not thinking about *that* sort of psychological model, but of more widely known ones with some popular appeal such as the Freudian one just discussed, or the one we shall discuss next based on the ethological model of man. As we consider this more popular model, however, we urge our readers not to forget that,

as a matter of plain fact, such popularly known models are not
the ones most widely used by research psychologists today.

Ethological models of man

The next model to be considered is chosen for several reasons.
First, it is a good example of the way in which ideas from other
related biological disciplines are put to work in psychology.
Second, it has received wide publicity in recent years through the
writings of Desmond Morris and others. Third, it is a good
example of the type of psychological theory which can be readily
extended beyond its appropriate domain so as to produce clear
conflicts with Christian beliefs about man and his nature. In such
a case it becomes extremely important to distinguish between the
validity and usefulness of the scientific model as such and the
invalid, unjustified speculations which are supposed to be derived
from it. The first the Christian psychologist accepts on the same
terms as any of his other scientific models: the second he refutes
as bad science and contrary to revealed Christian truth.

The pioneers of the approach to behaviour which gave rise to
this model were Lorenz and Tinbergen. They called themselves
ethologists and defined 'ethology' simply as the 'scientific study
of behaviour'. Ethologists, in contrast to most psychologists
claiming to be behaviourists, studied a wide range of animals,
including man, in near natural conditions. One of the distinctive
features of the ethologist's approach is his interest in understanding
what this or that piece of behaviour achieves for the animal
concerned. He wants to know what function some particular
behaviour fulfils in the life of an animal and what function it may
have fulfilled in the survival of the species. This kind of approach,
based as it has been on extremely careful and painstaking observation, has made it possible to specify, with some precision and
in considerable detail, the ways in which stimuli emitted by one
member of a species may evoke or inhibit particular forms of
behaviour by other members of the same or different species.
This leads to models of behaviour which talk in terms of sign
stimuli, of specific action patterns, of innate releasing mechanisms
and so on – all very familiar to psychology students. For the

benefit of the non-specialist reader, however, we may perhaps give a specific illustration from the now classical work of one of the leading ethologists, Professor Tinbergen of Oxford. Working with the three-spined stickleback, he discovered that certain stimuli in the environment of a male stickleback would evoke a quite specific sequence of behaviour, and that this behaviour was dependent upon such things as the time of the year, the temperature of the water, the length of the days, the particular state of the female at that time, whether her belly was enlarged, whether it was red-coloured or not and so on. He found that, by making suitable models with varying degrees of similarity to the female stickleback, he could define quite precisely what aspects of the female stickleback's form evoked the particular kinds of behaviour in the male stickleback, and vice versa.

This kind of investigation has also been carried out on higher animals and studies with non-human primates have also been reported. It is these latter studies which provide the starting-point for such popular ethological best sellers as *The Naked Ape* by Desmond Morris. As those familiar with *The Naked Ape* and similar books will know, a good deal is made of observed similarities between the expressive function of gestures amongst human and non-human primates. In both cases such gestures are used in communicating in a non-verbal way. A number of workers have pointed out that man shares a number of gestures and facial expressions with other primates, for example, the moving of the eyebrows and the use of a grin. Many primates, including man, grin as an expression of pleasure and at times of submission. Likewise the so-called 'open-mouth threat' of the protruding lips seems to be very similar in man and other primates. To some extent the same can be said of vocal sounds made by man and non-human primates, some of which seem to have a similar significance in both cases. For example, some kind of bark seems to signal alarm amongst gorillas, chimpanzees, baboons and rhesus monkeys. Screeching and screaming signify distress. Soft low-frequency sounds are made in situations where confrontation is occurring.

That these sounds often have similar significance for man is not difficult to observe, since we also tend to shout in alarm, to scream with fright and to growl with anger. To notice such similarities in behaviour, however, should not in itself cause any immediate problems from a Christian point of view. The evidence of such similarities is not itself a threat to the Christian position. They are analogous to the known similarities in physiological functioning between human primates and non-human primates which hitherto have not been thought to pose any particular threat to Christian beliefs about man. Indeed, we may be thankful that such similarities at the physiological level have provided an extremely important avenue for deepening our understanding of human physiology. Why, therefore, when one discovers certain similarities of behaviour between human and non-human primates, should one become unduly concerned from a Christian point of view?

To say this is not, in any sense, to accept the excessive and misleading accounts of man given in *The Naked Ape* and similar popular writings in recent years. There is no doubt that authors such as Desmond Morris have generalized far beyond the results of experiments and of observations based upon careful comparisons between human primates and non-human primates. This applies both to individual and to group behaviour. Likewise some have written speculatively without acknowledging the extent of such speculation and have made quite erroneous assertions about man's aggressive behaviour. Such extrapolations, far beyond the evidence, are more likely to cloud the real issues than to illumine them. This is not simply a matter of an issue between Christians and non-Christians, but at its basic level a matter of inappropriate extrapolations and abuse of scientific evidence. That this is the case is amply illustrated by the severe criticisms made, for example, of the work of Desmond Morris in *The Naked Ape* and of Konrad Lorenz in *On Aggression*[2] by other leaders in this field. Since, in *The Naked Ape*, Morris has gived the non-specialist reader the impression that his more speculative theories are closely linked with the core of reliable scientific observations from which he starts, it needs to be said that only a small fraction

[2] Lorenz, K., *On Aggression* (Harcourt, Brace and World, New York, 1966).

of his views are soundly based and an even smaller fraction uncontroversial. For example, in the name of scientific ethology he presents his readers with a salacious mixture of fantasy and speculation. No doubt some readers will, for personal reasons, be predisposed to accept what he has written. They should be warned, however, that the supposed factual bases from which he derives some of his most provocative (in every sense) ideas, are not only suspect but probably wrong. Thus, for example, on the question of sexual sign stimuli exhibited by the human female and reacted to by the human male, Eibl-Eibesfeldt,[3] a distinguished ethologist, and pupil of Lorenz, has commented, 'His (Morris's) thesis is hard to support, specially because more likely interpretations exist for the development of these releasers.' Eibl-Eibesfeldt's book contains a detailed refutation of Morris's thesis. He is not, of course, denying that, for example, the female breasts and lips have significance as sexual signals or releasers. His point is that Morris's particular interpretation is unsupportable from the available evidence.

As regards Lorenz's views expressed in his book *On Aggression*, these, together with R. Ardrey's book *The Territorial Imperative*,[4] have been subjected to searching criticism and refutation by a group of specialists in the same area of scientific enquiry and published collectively, under the title *Man and Aggression*,[5] edited by Ashley Montagu. For example, John Crook in his chapter 'The Nature and Function of Territorial Aggression', after discussing Ardrey's thesis, concludes that:

'By adopting a limited Lorenzian view of the nature of aggression Ardrey ignores most of the experimental ethological literature on the subject. Instead of resulting from an innate and ineradicable force demanding repetitive expression, aggressive behaviour occurs normally as a response to particular aversive stimuli and ceases upon their removal. The prevalence

---

[3] Eibl-Eibesfeldt, I., *Ethology – The Biology of Behaviour I* (Holt, Rinehart and Winston, New York and London, 1970), p. 437.
[4] Ardrey, R., *The Territorial Imperative* (Atheneum, New York, 1966).
[5] *Man and Aggression,* ed. Ashley Montagu (OUP, London, 1968).

of aggression in modern man may thus be attributed to aversive features in the complex over-crowded, over-competitive, over-stratified social world in which he lives rather than to some unsatisfied vital urge. In man, also, aggression is commonly associated with frustration born of the delay in responding imposed largely by his learning to play social roles in a community. There is every reason to suppose that individual sensitivity to stimuli likely to evoke aggression is determined during socialization. The manifestation of aggression in human society is thus largely a cultural attribute.'[6]

Likewise S. A. Barnett, in his discussion of Lorenz's widely read book *On Aggression*, comments:

'. . . I have read the book through more than once. On each reading more self-contradictions, confusions, and questionable statements have emerged. How much more acceptable would have been an unpretentious account of actual behaviour. It is sad that so much talent should have been misapplied in this fashion. As it is, since *On Aggression* is presented as authoritative at least on animal behaviour, it is liable to bring ethology into disrepute with critical readers, and also to mislead students and laymen. But the scope and implications of the book are far wider. It makes statements on two crucial features of our existence: the growth of social behaviour in children, and the prevention of violence and war. These are not topics in which loose thinking can be accepted with a tolerant shrug; such work should be based on a respect for facts, for logic and for the researches of others. Instead, the method of *On Aggression* is essentially anti-rational. This method should be repudiated by all scholars – indeed, by all responsible people.'[7]

This brief look at the ethological model has highlighted a number of important issues. As Christians we are committed by the God of truth to the search for, and adherence to, the truth.

[6] Crook, J. H., in *Man and Aggression*, pp. 172 f.
[7] Barnett, S. A., in *Man and Aggression*, p. 26.

Amongst other things this means that we cannot condone any extrapolations, no matter how distinguished the writer, which, as Barnett put it above, fail to respect 'facts, logic and the researches of others'.

Second, we must show up for what they are, the tendentious, propagandist extrapolations which go far beyond the available evidence. In this field the most obvious unjustified extrapolation is the assumption upon which Morris's *The Naked Ape* is based, that man is 'nothing but' an animal operating *only* at the level where comparison with other sub-human primates may indeed be justified. I am not denying that man may respond to sign stimuli and to expressions of aggressive and other behaviour in fellow men and women in ways which bear striking similarities to behaviour in non-human primates. The point I am making is that an account at that level is only one of a number of accounts of man that must ultimately be given if justice is to be done to the true complexity of man, his behaviour and his nature.

Here, then, we have yet another example of the fallacy of 'nothing-buttery' mentioned in chapter 2. In this case it consists of the assertion that, because man's behaviour in some of its aspects is explicable within the same conceptual framework developed to understand the behaviour of sub-human primates, therefore he is 'nothing but' this. The Christian view is that man does indeed manifest these intricate mechanisms in his inter-personal behaviour but that he is something much more than a collection of such mechanisms. What this 'something more' is comes partly from a recognition of the full complexity of his behaviour from a psychological point of view; and that is a story which we are only beginning just now to document carefully, as we shall show in a moment. For the Christian, however, his belief in this 'something more' comes primarily from what God has chosen to reveal about the nature of man. Man, he believes, has a significance and destiny over and beyond that given him as the crown of a process of psychological development of bewildering complexity. This he sees as the capacity for a relationship with God, as a son to a father. Once we start to write in these terms we move to a level of discourse at which it is proper to consider the biblical model of man as we find it contained in Scripture. Before doing that, however, we shall consider one further widely used model in contemporary psychology.

Skinner and behaviourism

This final model sits firmly in the behaviourist tradition of J. B. Watson and has received wide and, at times, controversial publicity in recent years through the writings of the American psychologist, Professor B. F. Skinner of Harvard. His influence is felt not only through his laboratory studies of learning but also through their many applications.

The basic idea with which Skinner works, and the method which he uses is, to quote the words of a book on behavioural control, 'no different in principle from one that Grandma might have elected, but is used more systematically.'[8] Starting from the fact that there are consequences of behaviour of all kinds, Skinner has systematically studied the ways in which, by manipulating them, behaviour can be shaped, established or got rid of. Writers in this field, following the terminology introduced by Skinner, regard the most influential shapers of behaviour as basically of two kinds. These are 'reinforcers', known to us more familiarly as rewards for actions, and 'punishers', consequences which are unpleasant in one way or another.

Skinner's contribution is that, as a result of his own and his colleagues' work over the last thirty years, we now understand much better how reinforcers and punishers shape and control behaviour, both of animals and of humans. One piece of psychological apparatus which bears his name is used to shape a rat's behaviour. By using a food reward a rat is brought near to a lever in a box. Before long the act of actually pressing the lever is associated with receiving food. Thereafter the animal will continue to press the lever and receive the reward as long as it is hungry. Skinner has studied very carefully the precise timing necessary between the pressing of the lever and the giving of the reward in order to produce and sustain a lasting behaviour change of this kind.

[8] London, P., *Behaviour Control* (Harper and Row, New York, 1969), p. 95.

Since this is not a textbook on psychology, it is not appropriate for me to go into any more detail here. The simple point I want to make is that this kind of 'shaping' of behaviour, known as 'instrumental conditioning' or 'operant conditioning', can be applied not only to the shaping of our own self-controlled behaviour, but also to the teaching of a variety of skills and to the efficient acquisition of some kinds of knowledge. The real problem is to have sufficient ingenuity to see how, in any given situation, the environment may be controlled in order to shape the behaviour in a required way and to maintain it, once it is shaped. Such behavioural shaping techniques are today used to train very complicated patterns of behaviour, as well as simple skills, so that, for example, many retarded and chronic psychotic patients in hospital wards have been helped by the use of such methods. In some hospitals a whole so-called 'token economy' has been introduced in order to 'shape' the behaviour of the patients in the hospital. Thus the key notion behind Skinner's work is that behaviour is shaped and maintained by its consequences. Once recognized, this can be used to control the interaction between an organism and its environment so as to establish or abolish particular behaviour patterns. In Skinner's own words,

'What all of this and that complicated verbiage means is we are studying the ways in which the consequences of behaviour are contingent upon what an organism is doing in a given situation.'[9]

At this point I must distinguish carefully between Skinner's scientific contribution and his speculative writings. It is in the latter that he freely imports his own values, beliefs, hopes and fears, but this importation should not detract from the importance of the former. Neither, of course, does his scientific contribution give any grounds for accepting his speculations about how the techniques he has devised might be applied in order to produce the idealized society. This he equates with the Utopia long sought by social and political reformers.

[9] Skinner, B. F., in *Firing Line*, a transcript of a programme dated 17 October 1971, p. 6.

Our immediate concern now, however, is with Skinner's psychological model. It is one of Skinner's basic contentions that we must not formulate psychological theories which involve non-observable, mentalistic entities. Perhaps it is for this reason that there has been little attempt by religious people to 'fit' their preferred theological model of man with Skinner's. So long as Skinner's model is evaluated on its merits as a contribution to our techniques for shaping and maintaining behaviour there is no conflict with Christian beliefs. Conflicts arise when unjustifiable extrapolations are made, such as that, because aspects of animal and human behaviour can be manipulated using their techniques, man is therefore 'nothing but' a stimulus-response machine. Skinner has not gone uncriticized by his psychological colleagues. Many feel that he fails to do justice to much of human experience and behaviour. It is one thing to be the world's most knowledge-able circus trainer, quite another to pretend that all man's achievements in art, literature, religion and science can be handled within the same explanatory framework. What then do we conclude about Skinner's psychological model? First, it is clearly an important contribution to our knowledge of how conditioning and learning take place. It has already been shown to have considerable potential in a number of applied fields, and its merits on these grounds must not be forgotten nor denied because Skinner goes on to make wild, excessive and totally unjustified extrapolations about the wider affairs of men and nations. Second, there is no obvious nor necessary conflict with Christian beliefs. These arise only when 'nothing-buttery' again rears its seductive head. It is one thing for Skinner to decide that the most productive strategy as a scientist is what is normally termed 'methodological reduc-tionism'; it is quite another to move on from that to claim that his scientific success as a methodological reductionist has any logical link with his personal philosophy of metaphysical reduc-tionism. Skinner's views on reductionism are discussed in greater detail in chapter 7.

Summing up
From this very brief consideration of four theories about how

man works psychologically certain things emerge. First, only those who are ignorant of what contemporary psychology is all about are likely to make an unqualified assertion such as that psychology conflicts with Christian views about man. Second, it is vitally important to ask of any statement made in the name of psychology, Is it supported by the relevant evidence? Is it part of the essence of the theory or is it the personal speculation and extrapolation of the maker of the statement? Third, because a theory makes sense of data from a circumscribed set of studies that does not mean that it can therefore be applied at once to all behaviour. Whether it can or not is itself an empirical question. Fourth, several of the supposed conflicts between psychology and Christian faith have arisen when unjustified extrapolations of particular psychological theories have been made far beyond the appropriate and proper context of application of such theories. In other words, we have the emergence of the 'nothing but' phenomenon outlined in chapter 2. Fifth, conflicts have arisen from time to time because of well-meaning but misguided attempts to 'fit' this or that psychological model of man with what is taken to be the Christian view of man and his nature. It is to this topic that we must now turn our attention.

4 The Christian view of man

Before I can say anything about how psychological accounts of man are related to Christian views of man, I must at least indicate, if only in general terms, what I take to be the main characteristics of the Christian view of man. That alone is my excuse for presuming, as a mere psychologist, to write about the Christian view of man. And, let me hasten to add, I am all too aware of the danger, let alone the impertinence, of allotting only a few pages to a topic which has occupied volumes of theological writing, has been the focus of discussion and debate at historic Church Councils and has been the subject of famous heresies. But if the relationship is to be explored, the task must be attempted. And incidentally, in writing of the Christian and the psychological views of man, I am not for one moment intending to deny that the Christian view enshrines some very profound human psychology. Rather, in this context, I am simply using the word psychology in its narrow, contemporary scientific sense, as spelled out in chapters 2 and 3. If that is borne in mind some unnecessary misunderstandings may, I hope, be avoided later on.

The biblical perspective
The first thing we notice is that the Christian view is in a sense timeless. It has made sense to men and women in all ages. That it conveyed important truths in pre-scientific eras should warn us against misconstruing it and its vocabulary by attempting to endow its familiar terms with a precision never intended. Un-

fortunately attempts have been made at times to ape what psychologists are doing and to produce from Scripture a model looking like the scientific ones.

The second thing we notice is that the Bible's emphasis is not upon man studying himself but upon God revealing a God-centred picture of man and his place in the world. It is, therefore, a view which starts with God, not with man, and one which is as much concerned with God–man relationships as with man–man relationships.

Third, the biblical view is for now; it is for facing the problems of today. It is for living, not for designing psychological experiments. As Welford put it,

'The psychological view represents a working hypothesis designed to co-ordinate the facts obtained from a large number of scientific studies and to guide the search for further facts. It is thus tentative, subject to frequent modification, and clearly incomplete in that it does not cover areas in which evidence is lacking.'[1]

By comparison, and by contrast, Welford characterizes the religious view of life as one that

'. . . aims at co-ordinating the common experience of ordinary men with the special experience of a few and the lessons of history, to provide an orientation towards the world and a guide to everyday life in it. As such it must be complete, in the sense of being able to provide some sort of answer to any question which arises in the course of daily living. The exigencies of moment to moment and day to day will not wait for a solution to be worked out to full scientific standards: man in his ordinary living cannot, like the academic psychologist, suspend judgment if evidence is lacking.'[1]

Fourth, the language of the Bible is not the language of contemporary, experimental science. The Bible does not talk about

[1] Welford, A. T., *Christianity – A Psychologist's Translation* (Hodder and Stoughton, London, 1971), p. 16.

human species, but about people; it is not biological but bio-graphical. It is not the properties of human beings whether physiological or psychological that are discovered in the Bible; it is the actions of men in history that are described.

Fifth, it is important to remember that the Bible is a library of books. As such, not only do we find different writers giving different slants on the same topic, thus enriching the whole, but we also find different authors at times using the same word in different ways or using different words for the same concepts. For example, Paul invariably uses *pneuma* for man's spirit, but hardly ever uses *psychē*. John, by contrast, never applies *pneuma* to man. This means that, in looking for a scriptural answer to our question, we must overcome the temptation to focus exclusively on one part of Scripture, such as Psalm 8 or the early parts of Genesis. A balanced picture of man can be achieved only by carefully comparing Scripture with Scripture whilst resolutely refusing to ignore those passages which do not easily fit into tidy models.

With these cautionary comments in mind, we turn now to ask what are some of the key features of the biblical picture of man? In doing so, and in looking for an answer to the question 'What is the Christian view of man?', it may be helpful to break down the problem into three subsidiary questions. First, What is man? in the sense of What is his calling? Second, How does Scripture encourage us to face the mystery of man and to conceptualize his many-sidedness – one who feels, thinks and acts? In other words, What is his nature? Third, What clues does Scripture afford to guide our answer to the question man has always asked himself: What, if anything, awaits him after physical death? What is his destiny? We shall look first at the teaching of the Old Testament before considering the more detailed treatment given us in the New.

Man's nature and calling: the Old Testament emphases
Most commentators point out that the Genesis narrative intro-duces two distinct features of the Hebrew ideas of man. They concern his nature and his calling. These themes are taken up

again in Psalm 8, another crucial Old Testament reference to man. As regards his nature, two aspects are held in delicate balance. On the one hand we have the majesty and mystery of man as the summit of God's creation; on the other hand we are reminded that man is himself part of creation, a hint never to forget his creatureliness.

In Genesis 1:26, 27 we read that God said, 'Let us make man in our image and likeness . . . So God created man in his own image; in the image of God he created him.'[2] Whilst it is here asserted that, in some sense, man is like God, we are not told in any detail what that means. We must therefore look elsewhere in Scripture for amplification. Since God is spirit the likeness is clearly not physical likeness.

Some commentators believe that man's likeness to God is to be found in his intellectual, moral, social, and spiritual capacities. They believe that in all these respects he is unique when compared with the animals. Others would argue (see later in this book, p. 92) that his uniqueness in regard to his intellectual, social, and perhaps even moral, capacities is quantitative rather than qualitative. Be that as it may, it is clear to me that, according to Scripture, man stands uniquely apart from animals in his spiritual capacity. The Bible clearly teaches that a man can enter into a deep personal and intimate relationship with God. In Genesis 3 God speaks to man. We are taught that God made man to enjoy and live in fellowship with himself. Thus in Genesis 3:8 we read, 'The man and his wife heard the sound of the Lord God walking in the garden at the time of the evening breeze.' As we shall see in a moment, this theme is taken up and developed in the New Testament account of man and his destiny.

The other noteworthy aspect of the Old Testament account of the nature of man, we said, was his creatureliness. In Genesis 1:27 we have the simple statement that 'God created man', followed in Genesis 2:7 by the amplification that 'God formed a man from the dust of the ground . . . man became a living creature'. This theme is taken up in Psalm 8 where man's creatureliness is highlighted

[2] The biblical references which follow are all taken from the New English Bible unless otherwise indicated.

when he is seen in the context of the greatness of the rest of creation. Thus we read in verses 3 and 4,

'When I look up at thy heavens, the work of thy fingers,
   the moon and the stars set in their place by thee,
   what is man that thou shouldst remember him,
      mortal man that thou shouldst care for him?'

Other references along this same theme are found, for example, in Genesis 3:19, 'Dust you are, to dust you shall return.' In Genesis 18:27 Abraham replied, 'May I presume to speak to the Lord, dust and ashes that I am.' And in Psalm 103:14 we read, 'For he knows how we were made, he knows full well that we are dust.'

The second distinct feature of the Hebrew idea of man concerns his calling, which is his lordship over creation. Both in Genesis 1 and 9, and in Psalm 8, man's appointed function in the universe is seen in his relationship to God to be as custodian of the earth, as God's vice-gerent. Thus in Genesis 1:26 we read that 'God said, "Let us make man in our image and likeness to rule the fish in the sea, the birds of heaven, the cattle, all wild animals on earth, and all reptiles that crawl upon the earth",' and again in Genesis 9:2 after the Fall, 'The fear and dread of you shall fall on all wild animals on earth. . . ; they are given into your hands.' This is a theme taken up in Psalm 8:6, 'Thou makest him master over all thy creatures; thou hast put everything under his feet . . .' Man is thus called to act as God's vice-gerent upon earth, as his steward, and to have and enjoy fellowship with his Creator.

As we turn to a more detailed consideration of the Old Testament teaching about man and his nature we are struck by the way in which, at different times, particular aspects of what is the mystery of man are taken up and developed. In reply to the question, What does it mean to be a person? the Old Testament writers draw attention to three special aspects of personhood. In the first place, to be a person is to be alive physically, to be a 'living creature', to be a tangible, material person. For this aspect of his nature the word *nephesh* is most consistently used, as, for example, in Genesis 2:7. It is usually translated 'soul'; but it is also, from time to time, rendered as 'life', or 'creature', or 'body' and, indeed, as if to warn us against trying to build too much into our definition, it is translated on one occasion as 'dead body'.

In the second place, the Old Testament recognizes that aspect of a person most apparent when he is acting and reacting. Although these reactions are not strictly tangible, nevertheless they arise out of contact with other persons, events and circumstances. Thus we are taught that meeting trouble makes men sad, the need to work makes man weary, riches when denied are capable of making men covetous. In such acting and reacting it is primarily the heart of a man which is referred to, and, to a lesser extent, his 'soul'. These two, 'heart' and 'soul', are thus, for these purposes, used interchangeably, so much so that it is not possible to differentiate consistently between them. Thus, on the one hand, we read in 1 Samuel 25:37 that 'his heart died within him', but in Job 10:1 'my soul is weary of my life' (RV). This aspect of personhood is not normally further subdivided to distinguish between, for instance, mind, will and emotions. Indeed, there is no separate Old Testament word for mind at all. When 'mind' appears in the English versions of the Old Testament it is normally a rendering of *nephesh* or *leb* or *ruach*, even though these three different words carry distinctive core meanings.

Having paid due attention to man's actions and reactions as a living person, the Hebrew Scriptures portray yet another aspect of man. This is an intangible quality which is nevertheless important and significant. The Hebrew writers note that a man's quality is, in a sense, more than the sum total of his actions and that he sometimes reacts other than in the manner which the circumstances surrounding him would lead one to expect. It is this intangible quality which is labelled the *ruach* or 'spirit' in the Old Testament. Whilst the word often denotes God's quality (the 'spirit' of God), it can be applied also to heathen man, as a reference to Deuteronomy 2:30 and 2 Chronicles 21:16 (RV) makes clear. It can also be equated with character, in our sense of the word; that is, the quality which we associate with a person, his wisdom or his folly, his humility or his pride. It is this spirit which shows what man is truly like and so, by implication, what the source of

inspiration for his living must be. See, for example, Proverbs
20:27.

It should be noted, at this point, that the Old Testament seems
to know nothing of a purely intellectual reaction to life. It seems
that the Word of God speaks to and is written upon the heart; it is
never given simply as academic information. From this it might
follow that the scientific quality of objectivity, which we prize so
highly, finds little place in Old Testament thought. Moreover,
the reaction that a man makes to events and circumstances of any
kind, whether he is considering kindness or persecution shown
by others, or viewing the creation in which he lives and of which
he is a part, is never regarded in the Old Testament Scriptures as a
dispassionate activity, but is seen as a total involvement, a total
reaction, whether it be of anger or of worship.

One other aspect of the Old Testament account of man is
noteworthy. Scholars have emphasized that, in Hebrew tradition,
what gives a man his 'weight', his honour and dignity, his glory,
is not his cleverness, nor even his wisdom, but his 'righteousness'.
And Hebrew righteousness is not simply morality but relationships supported by morality. With Jehovah the relationship of
favour or blessing comes through keeping his commandments.
Righteousness also encompasses right relationships within the
complex network of family, tribe and nation. Keeping the right
relationship in a state of balance is, for the Hebrew, *shalom* – peace
and well-being. Such righteousness comes from following the
guidelines laid down by God. Sin disturbs this state of divine 'law
and order', both in the individual and in society. And a sinner man
most assuredly is – which is another inescapable feature of the
realistic account of man in the Old Testament. Consider, for
example, Genesis 6:5, where we read,

'The Lord saw that the wickedness of man was great in the
earth, and that every imagination of the thoughts of his heart
was only evil continually. And the Lord was sorry that he had
made man on the earth, and it grieved him to his heart' (RSV).

Summarizing this brief look at the Old Testament cameo of

man we have seen that the realistic picture of man, given in Genesis and illustrated biographically time after time in Scripture, is that man, created in God's image, given custody of and lordship over creation, and surrounded completely by God's providential goodness, nevertheless incomprehensibly denied God obedience. Man was created to share the divine image and as a consequence also shared the divine rule. He was given dominion over the earth. But, tragically, through his disobedience, instead of behaving like God he behaved at times more like the beasts. Instead of exercising dominion he was himself defeated. Rather than subduing the creation he failed to subdue himself. Thus through man's disobedience the divine image was spoiled and his dominion was largely lost. As one commentator put it,

'Paradise is irreparably lost; what is left for man is a life of trouble in the shadow of a crushing riddle, a life entangled in an unbounded and completely hopeless struggle with the power of evil and in the end unavoidably subject to the majesty of death.'

And again,

'The manifold, profound troubles in human life have their root in the one trouble of man's relationship to God. Expressed more concisely, Genesis chapter 3 asserts that all sorrow comes from sin.'[3]

But we can add, thank God, the story does not stop there. Whilst that is the stark, realistic background of those who are without God and without hope, for the Christian there is a new and living way. For through Christ, man may recover both the image and the dominion that he has lost.

Finally, before leaving this all too brief and superficial look at the Old Testament account of man, we must remind ourselves that, whilst the terminology used to describe man, as outlined

---

[3] Von Rad, G., *Genesis* (1956), trans. J. H. Marks, 2nd ed. (SCM Press, London, 1966), p. 98.

above, may seem archaic, vague and lacking in the consistency and precision of contemporary science, it does nevertheless embody a lot of acute and permanently valid observations about man and his nature. We can prevent ourselves from seeing these only if we try to impose upon the biblical terms and thought-forms a degree of precision quite inappropriate to their nature.

Man's nature and destiny: the New Testament teaching

As we turn to the New Testament teaching about man we at once find a much more detailed treatment than anything in the Old Testament. Nevertheless, because the subject is dealt with so much more extensively, it does not follow that a correspondingly more precise picture is easy to construct. Anything but a superficial study soon makes it clear that the words of the text carry different meanings, in different contexts, and in the hands of different authors. It soon becomes evident that prolonged study is necessary before an integrated and coherent synthesis will emerge from these many and varied references to man. Any adequate study of this must take into account, not only differences in the use of the same words by different authors, but also the different cultures of the readers and the different purposes of the various documents. We are not competent to do this nor is this the place to embark on such a venture. For our purposes we wish to know what kind of a picture of man emerges from the New Testament teaching, what are its main features, and how are they to be related to the other models of man considered in the previous chapter? One may begin by making two generalizations. First, the New Testament clearly establishes that man is a unity, a psychophysical or psychosomatic unity. He is a unity, both in this present earthly life and in a new form in the new heavens and the new earth to which he looks forward. Second, although man is a unity, it is possible nevertheless to make valid distinctions between aspects of his functioning such as the physical and psychological, and in making these distinctions one derives greater insight into the nature of man.

In discussing man and in making statements about him, we find that the New Testament places man in a variety of frames of

reference or contexts. These are not exclusive but are complementary to one another, and each highlights different aspects of
man's nature. Three such frames can be identified. First, we have
the purely physical which is concerned with man as a living being.
Second, there is the psychological, loosely and non-scientifically
defined. This covers those aspects which describe the nature of
human life and the interrelationships of the components of man
(see, for example, James 2:26). To some extent, therefore, it
includes the first context. Third, we have the realm of the moral
and spiritual. This focuses both on the relationship between God
and man, and on that between one man and another. Within this
context, whilst the word 'heart' seems to be the focus of discussion, from time to time it centres also on the word 'conscience'.

The reason for identifying these different frames of reference is
that, by keeping them in mind, some of the seeming overlap and
complexity in the New Testament is considerably reduced because
different passages are now interpreted within their appropriate
frame of reference. Take, for example, the references to man as
flesh. It is all too easy to contrast the statement that he, that is
Christ, was manifested in the *flesh* (as we read in 1 Timothy 3:16,
which would be included in our first frame of reference) with 'all
flesh shall see the salvation of God' (Luke 3:6), which seems to be
an example of the second frame of reference, and also, with 'those
who are in the *flesh* cannot please God' (Romans 8:8) which refers
to the third frame of reference. Another distinction that emerges
from such a study is that the nouns for the components that make
up man are used in two distinct grammatical forms. At times they
are used as simple nouns, and at other times indirectly as adjectival
nouns. In this latter case they express the character or essence of
something. Examples are 'the *spirit* of your minds' in Ephesians
4:23, or 'the *imagination* of their hearts' in Luke 1:51. Certainly the
word 'spirit' is widely used in this form, for example in phrases
such as the 'spirit of' faith, fear, meekness, wisdom, truth and so
on. In this sense it bears a close and obvious resemblance to the
Old Testament *ruach*, 'spirit', referred to above.

As we bring together the Old and New Testament emphases

we may summarize the main features of the Hebrew–Christian view of man as follows. It enshrines a message for men in all generations. It tells man what is his calling, what is his nature and what is his destiny. He is called to worship and honour his Creator, to exercise a stewardship over the creation as a loving obedient son to a father, to enjoy fellowship with his Father Creator, whilst standing in awe of him as a creature to his Creator. He is encouraged to recognize the many-sidedness of his mysterious nature. He must hold in a delicate balance three aspects of his nature highlighted by Old and New Testament writers alike: his physical make-up; his capacity for mental life; and his capacity for making moral decisions, including an appreciation of the importance of a spiritual dimension to life. Working harmoniously together these are involved in maintaining a right relationship with God and with men.

A man's destiny depends upon how he responds to his Creator's invitation to enter into his spiritual inheritance. To do so he must recognize and accept his Creator's diagnosis of his true condition that he is by nature and by inclination a sinner – an unpalatable truth. He must accept that his Creator is also his Redeemer and that there is a remedy to match his diagnosis; a remedy, moreover, which is yet another expression of the love of his Creator; the one who ' . . . loved the world so much that he gave his only Son, that everyone who has faith in him may not die but have eternal life'. In short a man's true destiny is union with Christ. And that means fullness of life now and continuing life after physical death. We shall say more about this in a moment.

Man: the image of God

Before leaving this topic, however, we must take up again, but now with the New Testament record before us, the Genesis theme of man made in the image of God.

The truth that man is made in the image of God, which we noted in Genesis 9:6, and in Psalm 8, is taken up clearly in 1 Corinthians 11:7 where Paul asserts that ' . . . man is [note not *was* but *is*] the image of God', and by James who tells us that our fellow men 'are made in God's likeness', or image (James 3:9).

Now, however, the emphasis in the teaching about the image of God in man moves dramatically and decisively forward, for we are taught to refer this teaching directly to the person of the Lord Jesus Christ himself. Thus Jesus is the 'new man' (Ephesians 2:15 RSV; cf. 4:24); Jesus is the 'perfect man' (Ephesians 4:13 AV); Jesus is the 'last Adam' (1 Corinthians 15:45).

It is from Christ, who according to 2 Corinthians 4:4 is 'the very image of God', that there shines 'the gospel of the glory of Christ'. It is he who 'reflects the glory of God and bears the very stamp of his nature' (Hebrews 1:3 RSV). And, moreover, 'Just as we have borne the image of the man of dust, we shall also bear the image of the man of heaven' (1 Corinthians 15:49 RSV).

Several implications from the New Testament teaching about the image of God in man are relevant to our discussion here. First, that through union with Christ man may begin to recover the divine image which he has lost. The first man, made in the divine image, lost that image through his disobedience. Christ, the second Adam, gave a perfect obedience to God. His obedience led him to death; he died for our disobedience. But God raised him from death and exalted him to a position of supreme authority. In so doing, God gave to Christ the dominion that we through our disobedience had lost. In Christ, then, the image is restored and we can begin to regain the dominion over our sin and selfishness.

Thus, in Christ, man is still the lord and custodian of creation, but in an even fuller sense, as Hebrews 2:8, 9 reminds us, for 'we do not yet see everything in subjection to him [man]. But we see Jesus, who for a little while was made lower than the angels, crowned with glory and honour' (RSV).

This latter thought leads on to the most important thing that the New Testament, indeed the whole Bible, shows us about man. This is that *in Christ we see what manhood was meant to be*. It is only in Christ that man, in whom the divine image had been marred, can again become fully man, fully the image of God which makes a man a man. The New Testament also reminds us that, just as man's original creation in the image of God spelt out the equality of all men before God, so within the community of the new humanity there can be no division of race or class. Thus in

Colossians 3:10, 11 we read, 'You . . . have put on the new nature, which is being renewed in knowledge after the image of its creator. Here there cannot be Greek and Jew, circumcised and uncircumcised, barbarian, Scythian, slave, free man, but Christ is all, and in all' (RSV).

Man's destiny

So far we have considered two of the questions posed on page 66, *i.e.* What is man's nature? and What is his calling? The third was directed to problems which arise as we face up to the conviction that has possessed man in all ages that this life is not all there is. How do we explain the feeling, and often it is no more than that, that man is created for a life beyond this life, that the death of the body is not the end of the man? Certainly no discussion of the biblical view of man would be complete if nothing were said about the problems of immortality and of the nature of the body. This is a vast and controversial field, and we can do no more here than suggest some guide-lines to our thinking.

In recent years a number of writers have drawn attention to the pervasive influence of philosophical ideas inherited from the Greeks, particularly from Plato, which continue to permeate and distort Christian truth concerning the nature of man as an embodied creature. For many Greeks, death was a friend to be welcomed, since at death the soul would then be released from the prison house of the body and could move freely again, unrestricted by the confines of space and time. These views, when taken over by Christians, led to the belief that the body is a place where the remains of evil could be found within the Christian. This view led in turn to the belief that the body and its desires were therefore to be mortified, or at least ignored and starved, for they were truly a hindrance to the life of the soul.

This surrender of Christian teaching to predominantly Greek ways of thought could occur only by ignoring vast stretches of biblical teaching. According to Scripture, the body is as much a gift from God as the soul, and it is the body which is to be presented to God as a living sacrifice (Romans 12:1). It is to be the temple of the Holy Spirit (1 Corinthians 6:19) and it is both the spirit (or soul) and body, making up the whole man, which are to be wholly used in God's service (1 Corinthians 7:34; 2 Corinthians 7:1; 1 Thessalonians 5:23). Indeed, any careful study of Paul's argument in 1 Corinthians 6:12–20 underlines the importance the apostle attached to the role of the bodies of Christians as the 'limbs and organs of Christ' (v. 15), and as 'the shrine of the indwelling Holy Spirit' (v. 19). Moreover, a biblical account of what happens to a man after death cannot lead to the view that the soul survives in some disembodied form, but rather that the whole man, recreated in body, is to live anew. It is this new body for which the Christian longs, even in this present life (2 Corinthians 5:2). This new body will be a spiritual body, a glorified body, and no longer a physical and perishable body (1 Corinthians 15:44). In this new spiritual, glorified body, those who constitute the church of Christ will be presented to him as a bride to her groom, holy and without blemish (Ephesians 5:27).

These are important and encouraging truths for the Christian, particularly those growing old and seeing their bodily and mental capacities steadily decline. For they have the comfort and the assurance of looking forward to a new and incorruptible inheritance, an imperishable, glorified body. In this regard, the present writer remembers vividly how on one occasion he listened to, and participated in, a long and at times heated debate on the nature of the resurrection body, and how at the end an old, white-haired gentleman deflated all the speakers by the simple, yet confident and trusting comment, 'But what does it all matter anyway? We know that when he appears we shall be like him and what more wonderful prospect could anyone hope to look forward to than that?'

There is comfort here also for those who, as the next chapter recognizes, find within their present body tendencies (for example, homosexual ones) which prove difficult to restrain, for they also can look forward in confidence to the day when they will be without spot and without blemish. Such a view gives due recognition to the fact that the Hebrew–Christian view of man is as an intrinsic unity, a psychosomatic unity. All this, however, is not to be taken as denying that, in some sense, the soul must change its embodiment at death. Further discussion of this topic will be left until chapter 7, where we look more carefully at some of the implications of recent psychological thinking about how changes in the physical nature of man are reflected in his mental state and how some such physical changes are a normal part of the life history of all of us.

5 Relating psychological and Christian models of man

In the past it has sometimes been argued that, if it could be snown that the scientific, psychological model of man fits with the biblical model, then this would give added support to Christian belief as a whole, especially in an age of widespread unbelief. The motivation behind this way of thinking is understandable and the intention well-meaning. On closer scrutiny, however, it becomes evident that, on a number of grounds, such an approach is a mistake. In the first place it is based upon a misunderstanding of the nature of psychological models as they are constructed and used by psychologists today. As we saw in chapter 3 these models are made by man in order to make sense of the accumulated empirical and experimental data. By their nature, therefore, they change as more data come to light, causing them to be refined or, in some cases, totally rejected and replaced by new ones. In some cases, of course, as for example the 'information, processing' model of man described in chapter 3 which in some of its aspects can be expressed in terms of mathematical equations, it is very difficult to see just how one would go about trying to fit it to the Christian model of man. In other cases (and perhaps the Freudian model is a good example of this) it is easier to see how a model which uses terms which are loosely defined within an extremely flexible conceptual framework could, with a little ingenuity, be bent to fit what is thought to be the Christian model of man.

This happened in the 1930s and is in danger of happening again today. For example, as some Christians hear about ethologists' studies of man and how some of them describe him as 'innately aggressive', they find it natural to conclude that this is a justification for the Christian belief in man's fallen state, or, as some chose to call it, his innate depravity. But, as we have tried to indicate in chapter 3, the views put forward by some of these ethologists are seriously challenged by their scientific contemporaries and in some respects are now being shown to be almost certainly wrong. If you have made the grounds for your belief in the fallen state of man the passing theories of certain scientists, what becomes of your belief when the theories are changed or dispensed with?

To try to fit scientific models with the Christian model of man is, we believe, to misunderstand what they are all about. But it also reveals a misunderstanding of the Christian picture of man. As we have seen earlier, the picture of man that derives from Scripture is not one that is confined to any particular age, but embodies truths about man which are enduring and which apply in scientific and in pre-scientific eras alike. The Christian picture of man is one which makes sense of the common experiences of life in every age. Scientific models are deliberately limited in their scope and application.

Psychological models of man remain silent on questions of good and evil, sin, redemption, and eternal life – themes which are central to the Christian view of man concerned, as it is, with man in his relation to God, as he lives in a God-created but sin-ridden world. On this matter psychologists differ in their personal views. There are Christian psychologists and there are non-Christian psychologists. And, as we have mentioned several times already, Christian and non-Christian psychologists alike are found to be working right across the spectrum of current psychological research.

Psychologists' assumptions

Because it is a misunderstanding of both science and Christian faith to attempt to fit the models from the one with the models from the other, this certainly does not mean that we must ignore the implications of psychological views of man for Christian beliefs about man. Since there is no one accepted psychological view of man, however, it is necessary to pose the question in a slightly different way and to ask, Are there any features common to the variety of approaches used by psychologists today which have implications for, or conflict with, any fundamental Christian beliefs? We believe we can detect a number of such common features. Let us examine them in turn.

The first is that the understanding of human behaviour is helped by understanding animal behaviour. Not only is it easier, for obvious ethical reasons, to do controlled experiments on animals than on humans, but also, as we have indicated from time to time, the basic biological structure of the sub-human primate is so similar to that of human primates that a great deal can be learned about human behaviour by studying animal behaviour. This is made clear to students taking courses on the biological bases of behaviour. They are taught how some of the psychological functions studied in man may be clarified by comparable studies on animals. In particular, lectures in ethology and comparative psychology show how many of the basic behaviours of man (perceiving, learning, remembering, problem solving), as well as many of his emotional and instinctive reactions, can be profitably studied by looking at non-human primates and, in some instances, at animals considerably lower in the phylogenetic scale. There is nothing here which, in itself, conflicts with a Christian view of man. In so far as men and animals share common properties as regards their anatomy, physiology and biochemistry, it is not surprising that there are behavioural similarities also. There is nothing in this to conflict with such clues as we find in Genesis about men and animals. Conflicts arise only when unjustified extrapolations are made from such observed similarities. The uniqueness of man according to the Genesis narrative is not to be established on the basis of a distinction between the 'soulishness' of men and animals. Indeed, as we saw, precisely the same terms are used of animals and men in the creation story in this regard (*cf.* Genesis 1:24 with 2:27). The major emphasis, not only in Genesis but throughout Scripture, concerning the distinctiveness of being human is rather that man has the potential for a personal relationship with the living God, one of whose attributes is personhood. Men can come to know God in a personal way; herein lies the fundamental difference. There are no scientific grounds from behavioural studies of men and animals which could, by their nature, deny this central Christian belief. It is a truth to be spiritually discerned, not scientifically proved, to be validated in experience or suppressed in unrighteousness.

What then do we conclude? Do the study of animal behaviour and the discovery of close similarities between animal and human behaviour have any implications for Christian beliefs? We would argue not. Errors creep into our thinking only if we go on to believe that, because men share similarities in behaviour with animals, they are therefore 'nothing but' highly developed animals.

Another feature of the approaches used by most psychologists is the need to assume some form of determinism in setting about one's research. Put in its simplest form this means that the psychologist assumes that what he does one day under one set of conditions will be reproducible another day under the same set of conditions. Some would assume that what happens on the two occasions will be precisely the same (usually referred to as 'strong determinism'), and others that on the two occasions the outcome will be similar within close statistical limits (often referred to as 'weak determinism'). We shall give detailed arguments in chapter 6 for why we conclude that our freedom and responsibility are not diminished even if we regard the brain as a physically determinate system. We shall note there how easy it is for a student learning about mechanistic explanations of biological and psychological functions to begin to wonder whether, after all, man is 'nothing but' an extremely complex machine. Certainly the notion that there is a cause–effect relationship running through behaviour is not contrary to Christian belief. On the contrary, it strikes a familiar chord in Christian teaching that 'whatever a man sows he will also reap'. The fallacy lies in concluding that the obvious research benefits of the mechanistic approach to the study of behaviour necessitates the conclusion that man is therefore 'nothing but' a machine. That does not follow logically or scientifically and we would deny it on theological grounds.

Finally, there is a variant of the determinist approach which will be familiar to sociology students. In the context of their studies the point is not so much the determining influence of man's mechanistic make-up, as the cumulative effect upon him of all the environmental circumstances to which he is subjected and how these interact with his genetically blue-printed personality structure. The question is often then raised, Is man 'nothing but' the end product of such environmental pressures acting upon his genetic endowment? Again the error lies in the way the question is formulated.

'Nothing-buttery': a recurring theme

You will have noticed that in formulating these various questions we have listed the problems which contemporary behavioural sciences are said to raise concerning man and his nature. In each case we have shown that the problem may be formulated so as to suggest that man is 'nothing but' a complex animal, a complex machine, or the result of environmental forces. We have highlighted this aspect of each of these problems in order to see the issues more clearly. Nothing whatever is to be gained by trying to deny that there are advantages, from the point of view of research strategy, in regarding man as a complex machine. There is nothing to be gained by denying that, in some sense, man shares features of his behaviour with other animals, and that we may learn something about man from the study of animals. It is likewise undeniable that, within limits, the behaviour that a man shows at any given time is heavily dependent upon the circumstances in which he has developed, both in terms of the wider culture and the narrower family and social circles. But, as we saw in chapter 2, the advantages of such approaches do not constitute grounds for asserting that man is therefore 'nothing but' each of these things. We saw there how psychologists today readily accept the necessity for a multi-aspect approach to the understanding of behaviour. What is learned from each of these different approaches contributes its distinctive share to solving the problem of understanding a creature so complex as man. There is nothing here which of itself conflicts with a Christian approach to the study of man. Indeed, as we saw, the biblical teaching about man likewise emphasizes what we may call the multi-aspect approach to man.

Man's basic problem: a biblical diagnosis

We have said several times that the Bible's starting-point for its view of man is with God himself and that some of the most important features of the biblical model of man, that he is a sinner and needs forgiveness, are nowhere to be found in psychological models of man. We must now say a little more about the status of such non-psychological assertions about man's nature, since it is an area which worries a lot of Christians looking at the psychological model of man alongside the biblical model. Since the Bible's view of man is a God-centred one, its emphasis is upon the fact that man is made by God for a family relationship of a son to a father. The Bible also teaches that, by nature, we are not keen on this relationship. There is within us a natural tendency to want to keep our own hands on the controls of our lives. It is this obsession with keeping our hands on the controls and going our own way, regardless of what God has said, which is the basis of what the Bible calls sin. It is this all-pervasive tendency which, according to the Christian view, must be dealt with if man is to live in the way that God intended him to.

It is important here to realize that this is something that goes very deep. It asserts that natural man takes up a rebellious posture towards God at the deepest level. This posture is not to be seen solely as the aggregate of a lot of particular anti-social acts. These are merely symptoms of the deep underlying condition. There is nothing in the Bible to dissuade us from searching for the psychological causes of such anti-social acts. The Bible's diagnosis of our basic condition is at an altogether deeper level. Using our God-given talents, we may hope progressively to uncover what the psychological or indeed the physiological causes of this or that particular anti-social act are likely to be. The fact that there is a spiritual something that has gone wrong does not by any means imply that no natural explanation is therefore possible. What the Bible says is that it is according to our nature that we sin, and this leads us to expect that there will be causal chains accounting for our behaviour. This in no way conflicts with the Bible's account. It is complementary to that account and points to the fact that such anti-social acts are sin's natural outworking.

In this sense, social psychology is not to be regarded as a rival to what the church is doing and teaching. The suggestion has sometimes been made that scientists might eventually find a remedy for 'sin'. This implies that, ultimately, we, as scientific psychologists, will be able to deal with the problem of sin which Christians assert can be dealt with only by God acting in Christ. The answer we would give to the question this raises is that it is our job, as psychologists, to bend our energies to try to find a remedy for the anti-social behaviours which are the symptoms of our condition as sinners. In this way we can help to lessen to some extent the personal and social hurt which results from such behaviour. In this respect, we have a situation which is analogous to the contributions of researchers in physical medicine. Because Christians researching in medicine believe that, ultimately, all sickness and suffering entered the world through sin, it does not prevent them from bending all their energies as scientists to discovering the causes of physical illness and to relieving suffering wherever possible. Likewise, some forms of anti-social behaviour, properly regarded as sinful actions, may well arise because of the abnormal functioning of the human brain. For example, it now seems clear that some kinds of aggressive behaviour exhibited by certain criminals may be explicable at the level of the mis-functioning of the machinery of the brain. Where we can identify breakdowns at this mechanical level we should do all we can to put them right; but this will not deal with the problems at much deeper levels of the selfishness of mankind and his desire to go his own way rather than God's way.

There is a problem to be faced and dealt with at the level of the relation of a man to his Creator if the root of the symptoms which follow from the condition of sin is to be reached. It is true that, as psychologists, we may be able to provide a battery of techniques which will help in manufacturing new patterns of behaviour, some of which may look Christian. But, whilst the Bible is intensely concerned about behaviour, it is also concerned with more than that. God starts and continues his work at this totally different and more fundamental level. He is not the manufacturer of techniques, but he is the Creator and Sustainer of the whole show, and it is the clear assertion of Scripture that, when a man becomes a Christian, something so radical takes place that it is best described as being created as a new creature. Indeed, it says, he is a 'new creation in Christ' when he beomes a Christian. In this sense becoming and being a Christian is not simply manufacturing a new pattern of behaviour; it is not believing a new set of stories; it is not, as some try to pretend, entering a new world of make-believe. Rather it is, at the deepest level, becoming a new creation in Christ and entering into a living, personal relationship with him.

Note to the reader: Those who are eager to know what to make of some psychologists' descriptions of conversion as brain-washing and of belief in God as wishful thinking may wish to turn now to chapters 8 and 9. The problems discussed in chapters 6 and 7 could be regarded as rather more academic. As such they are likely to be of most interest to students taking university courses in psychology.

6 From animal to human behaviour

In this chapter we consider in more detail three issues raised in our review of psychological models in chapter 3. From time to time it has been asserted that each poses special problems for anyone holding Christian beliefs. The first concerns the implications of studies of animal behaviour for our assessment of man. It has been asked, In what sense is man different from animals and wherein, if at all, does his uniqueness lie? The other two issues arise from extensions and applications to the field of human behaviour of the work of Skinner and others on the control and manipulation of animal behaviour.

It seems to me undeniable that the study of animal behaviour has already greatly increased our understanding of human behaviour. There are, for example, the results of research into how behaviour is mediated through the normal functioning of the nervous system. This includes studies of the biochemical, physiological and neurological bases of behaviour. In addition, our knowledge of such basic psychological processes as learning and conditioning has been greatly increased by studies using animals. Following common practice in scientific investigation, it is sensible to start by trying to understand the simpler behaviour of lower animals. Building upon the findings from such studies, one can then move on to the study of the higher animals and the almost bewildering complexities of human behaviour.

In many psychological experiments it is important to know as much as possible about the genetics and the life history of one's subjects. In that way we can exercise the maximum possible control over factors which may be important determinants of the behaviour one is studying. Whilst such control is usually not possible with human subjects (for obvious ethical reasons), it is possible with laboratory-bred animals.

At times problems arise in psychology – concerning the effects of early blindness, for example – in which clues from human studies can be systematically followed up only by using animal subjects. At other times, hints may arise from the study of animal behaviour which alert us to the possible importance for human behaviour of hitherto unsuspected factors. One example of this would be the study of imprinting and the importance of mother–infant bonds formed very early in life.

Clearly animal behaviour is not only worth studying in its own right, but it can also greatly enrich our understanding of human behaviour. Dangers arise, however, when the over-enthusiastic use of a single species, such as the laboratory rat, threatens to divert us from the study of important aspects of complex human behaviour. Likewise, we find ourselves in trouble of our own making if we give way to the temptation to over-generalize the findings from one species to another species, whether animal or human, which show markedly different behaviour. Even where there are apparent similarities between species we have to remember, as Robert Hinde has emphasized, that these may be the result of parallel adaptation to the environment. The comparative method must be used with caution, and that entails selecting for initial comparison those species believed to be closely related phylo-genetically. Even then we may be easily misled. For example, until recently it was confidently claimed that the silent, bared-teeth display in apes could be compared with smiling in humans, and the play-face of the monkey with human laughing. It is now clear that the silent, bared-teeth display indicates fear and not contentment or amusement. Since other instances of unjustified and misleading extrapolations from animal to human behaviour were discussed in some detail in chapter 3, we shall not develop the topic here.

Men and animals: similarities and differences

Christian students sometimes get the impression that psychologists with Christian sympathies emphasize the differences between men and animals whilst those with non-Christian or anti-Christian beliefs underline the similarities. This may happen from time to time but, as a generalization, such a statement does less than justice either to the evidence or to the conclusions of careful scholars in the field. We may illustrate this by referring to the writings of two distinguished contributors to this topic. The first is Professor W. M. O'Neil, formerly Professor of Psychology at Sydney University, and the second, Professor W. H. Thorpe, Professor of Animal Behaviour at Cambridge University. Professor O'Neil does not write from Christian presuppositions; nevertheless, in a recent lecture, after pointing out that 'Man shares with the other animals many activities and functions', he went on to contend that there are ' . . . phenomena in respect of which man seems to be distinguishable from the other animals or to be peculiar or even unique'.[1] O'Neil lists the activities and functions that man shares with other animals as

'sensory discrimination, perceptual judgment, learning (perhaps in several forms), activation by stimuli and by various internal conditions (endocrine and other), locomotion, social interaction, reproduction, growth and death, sleeping and waking and so on.'

The four differences he identified were '. . . first . . . to do with conceptualization, the second with language, the third with value systems and the fourth with the person, self, or ego'. He pointed out that 'one may find evidence of some or all of these in embryonic form in other animals, especially in other primates'. He also commented that 'in some of these the differences may be no more than marked differences in degree, whereas in others the differences may be differences of kind'.

It is interesting to compare Professor O'Neil's summary with the conclusion that Professor Thorpe arrived at after comparing,

[1] O'Neil, W. M., *The Australian Psychologist*, Vol. 7, No. 2, 1971, pp. 72–89.

as he put it, 'the minds of animals and man'. Starting from a theistic viewpoint he wrote,

> 'We see, then, that in perception, in concept formation and in curiosity and exploration, the human mind seems to be essentially similar to, and to be the direct outcome of, the animal mind.'[2]

He further points out that, in the past, some have argued that what we call artistic experience and the artistic sense provide a real distinction between animals and man. But, he asks, does the evidence really support that view? Referring to the study of bird song, in which, of course, Professor Thorpe is an acknowledged expert, he asserts that

> 'the latest techniques of sound recording and analysis provide *prima facie* evidence that singing transcends the level of practical utility in a few species and perhaps constitutes the first steps towards true artistic activity'.[3]

Thorpe also considers that

> 'there is about . . . chimpanzee paintings an elementary sense of form, something of a unity of conception and of colour contrast, something also of a sense of balance – which forces us here again to grant a *prima facie* case for describing the work as artistic'.[3]

And he concludes, 'Therefore I believe we cannot, on the grounds of artistic sensibility, make a hard and fast distinction between the animal and the human mind.'[4]

Continuing his search for 'clear evidence of the difference between the mind of animals and men', Thorpe thinks he finds it in 'the act of knowing'. In this respect, when men are compared

[2] Thorpe, W. H., *Biology, Psychology and Belief* (CUP, London, 1961), p. 38.
[3] *Ibid.*, p. 39.
[4] *Ibid.*, p. 40.

with animals, there is 'a difference in the degree to which the symbol becomes freed from the subject so as to become manipulatable as part of an intellectual world'.[5]

It is noteworthy that O'Neil seems to be making essentially the same point when, in elaborating the first and second of his differences, he writes,

'The other animals provide clear evidence of communicating with one another but they seem to do so mainly through signals and perhaps not at all through symbols. The signals may be communicating such messages as "Come on", "Make off", or "Make yourself inconspicuous", but they never seem to communicate such messages as "Snow is white", "God's in his heaven", "Two and two make four", "You're a liar" or "You are the most wonderful girl in the world", because such messages require a degree of conceptualization and symbolization of which man alone (provided he is not a low-grade) seems capable.'[6]

Thorpe concludes that there is a difference between the minds of humans and of present-day animals in that humans are capable of 'a recognition of abstract moral law, eternal values which are in themselves good, and which must be the basis of Polanyi's "moral passions"'. Here, then, Thorpe thinks we have reached 'a distinction which we can, for the time being at least, regard as fundamental'. In summing up he later concludes,

'There is, in the highest aspirations of man in expressing the ineluctable universal obligation to seek and know ever higher levels of perfection, to comprehend even more perfectly absolute values, something *which far transcends* anything we have reason to believe exists in animals.'

'We cannot say that it is not there; for all we know, the brain of a wolf or a whale may be the centre for highly articulate and elaborate mental life in the strict sense of the word. But we

[5] *Ibid.*
[6] O'Neil, W. M., *op. cit.*, pp. 72–89.

have no evidence in favour of, and an immense amount of circumstantial evidence against, such a conclusion.'[7]

I think that a fair summing up of the views of most writers on the behavioural differences between animals and men would be that they regard them at least as differences of degree. The degree of difference is, however, so great in some instances (*e.g.* language ability, ability for conceptually complex thought, the formulation and application of moral principles and value judgments) that it may be argued that it is more accurate and more meaningful to regard them, as both Thorpe and O'Neil seem to do, as fundamental, qualitative differences, rather than merely quantitative ones. Having said that, I find it difficult to share the view sometimes expressed that there is something theologically at stake in being able to demonstrate such qualitative differences. I find it misplaced zeal to try to establish, for example, that animals can only learn whereas humans can think. If to think is, at least in part, to solve problems then animals can certainly do that to quite a sophisticated degree.

The point at issue here, however, is not to debate the particular question of whether or not animals can think, but rather to ask what is behind the search for differences in the psychological functioning of animals and men? Often, it seems, there lurks the belief that discovering such differences in some way underpins a Christian view of man. I see no grounds for this. Rather, as I have argued in chapter 3, whilst the search for such differences may be a worth-while psychological research project in itself, there are no theological stakes in the outcome. Man's essential difference rests in his capacity to respond to God his Creator in a personal way and in so doing to know a new fullness of living now and to inherit a life which does not end at physical death.

Behaviour control and modification

The basic laboratory techniques devised by Professor B. F. Skinner have been developed and extended so that today a whole new technology for the control and modification of behaviour is

[7] Thorpe, W. H., *op. cit.*, 44, 45, 47 (my italics).

available. Encouraged by the early successes achieved using a wide variety of behaviour modification techniques, Skinner has described how he believes they can be harnessed to shape the future of our society. He has presented these views in a highly speculative book *Beyond Freedom and Dignity*.[8] This has generated strong reactions from Christians and non-Christians alike who have been rightly concerned about the danger of unethical manipulations on a wide scale. First, therefore, we shall discuss Skinner's views on behaviour control as presented in *Beyond Freedom and Dignity*. We shall follow that with a wider discussion of some of the ethical and moral problems raised by rapid developments in behaviour modification techniques generally, including Skinner's.

One recent reviewer commented thus on the extent of Skinner's influence:

'He inspired the teaching machine and programmed learning. A worldwide movement of professionals practise his control devices upon thousands of retardates, homosexuals, phobics, soldiers, convicts, communards, the mentally ill and ordinary pupils in ordinary public schools.'[9]

With any such wide application the question must at once be faced of who decides what values shall set the goals towards which the behaviour-shaping techniques are directed. This important issue can all too easily be glossed over, especially when it is tacitly assumed that everyone knows and agrees what the aims of society are, as if there were one agreed 'ideal society' towards which all men are working. The moment one refers to an ideal society one immediately raises a key issue highlighted by Skinner's more speculative writings. We may put it this way: since, on Skinner's view, in any society, behaviour is being shaped and controlled, who shall do the shaping and controlling? Or put more simply still, who shall control the controller?

[8] Skinner, B. F., *Beyond Freedom and Dignity* (Alfred A. Knopf, New York, 1971; Jonathan Cape, London, 1972).
[9] Harris, T. G., 'The B. F. Skinner Manifesto', *Psychology Today*, August 1971, p. 33.

Posing the issue bluntly in this way points up other problems. For example, are the controllers to be scientists, and if so, what if the scientists, presumably behavioural scientists, differ amongst themselves about what are the ideal goals to which the society should be directed? Who shall then arbitrate between conflicting goals? The moment questions of goals are introduced, value judgments also enter. The values of behavioural scientists are not uniform. When the values of one behavioural scientist differ from those of another behavioural scientist, who is to decide which values shall be the ones which determine the goals towards which behaviour shall be shaped, modified and controlled by the techniques produced by the researches of Skinner and these self-same behavioural scientists? Not surprisingly, this latter point has been seized upon by most of the reviewers of Skinner's book *Beyond Freedom and Dignity*. As we consider it now we shall continue to bear in mind the need to keep separate the ethical and moral issues raised by his speculations and any evaluation we make of Skinner's contribution as a behavioural scientist.

A number of those who have reviewed Skinner's book have pointed out that, if it is to be taken seriously at all, it raises at least two key issues. The first, as we have already noted, is Who controls the expert behavioural controller? The second is, What relevance does the kind of explanation of behaviour, which it is possible to offer within the framework of a Skinnerian approach based upon schedules of reinforcement, bear to other approaches which might be given to the same set of data by, for example, the biochemist, the physiologist, the anatomist or the person who is himself being subjected to Skinnerian behavioural analysis? One other issue which, though incidental to the main theme of his recent book, is certainly relevant to this book is, How we are to evaluate Skinner's interpretation of the psychological function of religious practices? We shall deal with that in the next chapter.

The first point that should be made is that it is untrue to say that Skinner has not himself realized the importance of the question of who controls the controller. Indeed on page 102 of his book he writes,

'For whom is a powerful technology of behaviour to be used? Who is to use it? And to what end? We have been implying the effects of one practice are better than those of another; but on what grounds? What is the good against which something else is better?'

And on the following page he continues,

'A more useful form of the question is, "If a scientific analysis can tell us how to change behaviour, can it tell us what changes to make?" This is the question about the behaviour of those who do in fact propose to make changes.'

And in answer to the question, 'What values are to guide the choice of goals towards which behaviour shall be directed by the controller?', Skinner has a simple and as some would say, a simplistic, answer, namely that

'Survival is the only value according to which a culture is eventually to be judged, and any practice that furthers survival has survival value by definition'.

That the culture which survives may be tyrannical, bestial, or brutal seems of no concern to Skinner. Indeed, he clearly foresees different cultures having different features depending on what they regard as good. If cannibalism is good, then it will, for that group, be reinforcing and be maintained. He writes,

'What a given group of people calls good is a fact; it is what members of the group find reinforcing as a result of their genetic endowment and the natural and social contingencies to which they have been exposed. *Each culture has its own set of goods, and what is good in one culture may not be good in another*.'[1]

It is clear from this and other passages that cultural relativism is the order of the day for Skinner and any notion of revealed

[1] Skinner, B. F., *op. cit.*, p. 128.

standards of right and wrong, or good and evil, is anathema to his way of thinking. Here there is a clear conflict between Skinner and the Christian. But such a conflict has nothing to do with scientific fact or scientific evidence. It is a matter of personal values not in any way logically tied to, or derivable from, Skinnerian or any other principles of learning.

Skinner claims to deal with the issue of who shall control the controller when he says that the behaviour of those who exercise control is generally governed by the behaviour of those controlled more than by anything else. Another distinguished and controversial figure in American psychology, O. H. Mowrer, took issue with Skinner on this when he wrote, 'Suppose the scientists exercising control differ amongst themselves on what is good for the masses?' He significantly points out that 'A recent issue of the *Atlantic Monthly* carried a feature story on Skinner in which the author quotes him as having written (in one of his innumerable "day books" or "diaries"): "It may all be up to me." ' Mowrer comments, 'It has been said that "one gets mad if one goes too far alone".' He believes that Skinner seems to arrive 'at a theory of political dictatorship which seems to be conditioned more by personal predilection than by logical necessity'.[2]

The question of ethical values and goals is a recurring one in Skinner's writing and nowhere is it clearly resolved. In one recent debate of Skinner's views between H. H. Halsey and H. R. Beech[3] Halsey asked, 'Exactly how is it that Skinner tries to derive ethical statements from scientific ones?' And the answer he gave was that, 'He does so by an appeal to evolution. What he puts forward quite plainly is the ethical statement that what has survived,what is here now, is good. . . . and that seems to me', said Halsey, 'to be a completely indefensible position. Why should one assume that the evolved condition of man so far is a better state of affairs than that which existed several generations before?'

Later Halsey raised the question again, pointing out that most discussions from Skinner's side continued to hedge round the

[2] Mowrer, O. H. in a review of Skinner's book in *Contemporary Psychology*, 1972, Vol. 17, No. 9, p. 470.

[3] 'Mechanistic Man – a dispute between H. H. Halsey and H. R. Beech concerning Behaviourism and B. F. Skinner', *The Listener*, 20 April 1972, pp. 513–515.

question, How do we decide where we want to go? It seems clear
that Professor Skinner is a man who has a conception of what the
good life and the good world should be like, but the question is,
Where did he get that conception from? In this same debate,
Beech, supporting Skinner's viewpoint, agrees with Halsey's
criticism and concedes that 'the major weakness of the book is,
who is to be the contingency manager, the person who is going to
decide where society goes, what things to preserve, and what
things we are to dispense with'. Beech himself then goes on,
however, blithely to brush this issue aside by saying, 'Supposing
we could agree upon certain aims which society might reasonably
have, then here is a technology which would facilitate the
achievement of these aims.' But that, of course, is a very big
supposition. Indeed, the issue cannot be brushed aside, because
the fact is that men *do* differ radically in their suppositions concerning what should be the aims for society today. Perhaps
Halsey's assessment is the most charitable one can arrive at. He
points out that Skinner is ethically naïve in that, to quote Halsey
again, 'he trivializes the character of social interactions and even
trivializes the character or at least the complexity of what happens
inside of man.'[4] It is not enough for Beech to make the rejoinder,
'Man is psychological. He is not political, he is not economic and
he is not sociological; he is psychological.'

Such blatant 'nothing-buttery' at once leads on to the second
major issue raised by Skinner. How are accounts of behaviour,
framed in terms of schedules of reinforcement, related to accounts
which may be given in physiological terms or in terms of any
other biological science? And how are such spectator accounts
to be related to the actor accounts given by the individuals being
studied?

It is not easy in fact to discover to what extent Skinner really
is a metaphysical, as well as a methodological, reductionist. It is
true that some of those who have reviewed his book have
asserted that Skinner 'begins as a methodological reductionist –
one who concentrates on behaviour and its environmental

[4] *Ibid.*

determinants as a means of gathering data of an empirically covariant nature – but with his first methodological success he can convert rapidly to metaphysical reductionism.'[5] Other reviewers were less sure that Skinner was a convinced metaphysical reductionist. Thus W. Day went to some lengths to make the point that it is a philosophical mistake to regard what Skinner refers to as 'translations' as instances of philosophical reduction. It is Day's view that Skinner's translations are not examples of metaphysical reductionism.[6]

Since this is a point which we shall be taking up in some detail in chapter 10 when we consider Skinner's view that '. . . the good personified in a God does represent those things which we find reinforcing', and that '. . . men have evolved a conception of God . . . which can be reduced to what we find as positively reinforcing', we shall not do more than foreshadow the conclusion that we reach there, namely that, when pressed, it does seem that Skinner must be regarded as a metaphysical reductionist.

When challenged to explain why he was not committing the error of reductionism, Skinner readily agreed that the mechanics of how a person comes to know God, which is a proper study for the scientific study of religion, could not on logical grounds possibly refute the reality of the God believed in by the man who was being studied at the time. Dr Day in his review in *Contemporary Psychology* referred to above, takes up this point when he says,

'the book (*Beyond Freedom and Dignity*) simply does not deal with issues that threaten in the least what people are actually doing when they concentrate in their lives on activities that they regard as robustly meaningful in a spiritual or even a religious sense.'

It is one thing to talk in terms of contingencies of reinforcement and of aversive stimuli about how a man has come to know God.

---

[5] McCall, R. J., Special invited review, 'Beyond Reason and Evidence: The Metapsychology of Professor B. F. Skinner', in *Journal of Clinical Psychology*, Vol. 28, April 1972, pp. 125–139.
[6] Day, W., *Contemporary Psychology*, Vol. 17, September 1972, Number 9, pp. 465–468.

That is an explanation at a mechanistic level. It is quite another to pretend that nothing more remains to be said. On the contrary, there still remains the question of the significance of the experience of 'coming to know God' in terms of a God to be reckoned with.

Behaviour control technology: some ethical and moral problems

In his recent book *Behaviour Control*[7] Dr Perry London defines behaviour control as the ability to get someone to do one's bidding. He claims that whereas, in the past, efforts directed towards such ends were 'gross and tedious in their application and clumsy or unsure in all their effects' (p. 4), now 'all this is changing, and means are being found, in all crafts and sciences of man, society and life, that will soon make possible precise control over much of people's individual actions, thoughts, emotions, moods, and wills' (p. 4). He concludes that 'when the facts of today's behavioural technology are assembled and put in context, some people may be surprised at the extent to which it is now possible to manipulate people systematically. And it is petty compared to what will soon be possible.' The resources he has in mind include the techniques of psychotherapy and studies of the biochemical and neurological substrate of behaviour. Today the latter include, on the one hand, the development of a host of tranquillizing and energizing drugs and, on the other hand, the control of epileptic seizures, sexual desire and speech patterns by devices implanted in the brain and varied by remote radio control. On the credit side, he believes that the possible benefits of such scientific advances may be the elimination of mental illness, crime and even war. On the debit side, such developments pose a threat since they provide tools for the repression of freedom and the destroying of initiative.

The sum total of this ever-growing armoury Dr London refers to as 'behaviour control technology'. Such a technology he regards as 'scientifically inevitable, socially necessary, and psychologically prepared for'. Such a clear, and as some would say, exaggerated statement of the position certainly serves to alert one to some of

[7] London, P., *Behaviour Control* (Harper and Row, New York, 1969).

the ethical and moral issues which arise as the behavioural and biological sciences progress. Depending on one's viewpoint, every new advance will be received with deepening pessimism or expanding optimism. How should the Christian view such a situation? Before we attempt an answer to that question, let me emphasize just how many and varied are the kinds of behaviour already studied and, at least partially, controlled by just one of the weapons in the armoury of behaviour control technologists, namely, psychotherapy. I give these details for the benefit of the non-psychologist reader who may not be aware how far advances have already gone in this field. Such readers will then be able to sympathize a little more with the psychology student who first meets this information in one or more of his university courses.

The issues often first arise in courses on learning, where the work of Skinner figures largely. As we saw, for more than thirty years now Skinner has concentrated his researches upon arriving at a precise understanding of how behaviour is systematically changed by rewards and punishments. Such findings, stemming principally from studies of rats, can also be applied to the behaviour of monkeys, children and men. When this is done it is found that human behaviour can indeed be both shaped (*i.e.* the response brought to conform to what the experimenter has in mind) and maintained or extinguished with appropriate schedules of reinforcement. This, if you like, is the use of the prize and the cane, long familiar to schoolmasters, but now refined to the nth degree. Such developments have already proved effective when applied to problems which arise in training sub-normal children. There has been success also in accelerating the learning of some school subjects through programmed learning, and in giving patients control over undesirable behaviour, for example, in the treatment of alcoholics and homosexuals. The particular issues raised by behaviour therapy will be dealt with separately and briefly in a subsequent section since they pose special problems for psychologists in training.

Just how extensive is the range of conditions helped by these techniques is well illustrated by a further quotation from Dr London's book. He writes:

'The most common psychotherapeutic problems involve some aspect of the victim's behaviour which seems to be out of control, either from his own point of view or from that of some other presumably responsible people. The inability to refrain from drinking too much or from taking certain kinds of drugs, to restrain sexual impulses or to express them; to concentrate on school work; to stop ruminating over trivia; to learn to read properly; not to wet the bed at night; to free oneself from an over-dependent attachment to parents; to assert one's rights; to refrain from anti-social aggression or to express appropriate hostility; to get along with one's wife or to seek a well-earned divorce; to be free of groundless anxiety; to quell irrational fears of remote, unlikely, or harmless events; to be able to feel good; to shake oneself free of despondency or to come down from an endless, manic 'high'; to keep physical equanimity in the face of stresses, which raise fits of asthmatic strangulation or scale one's skin or cover it with hives or knot one's stomach into ulcerous aches; to move one's limbs, paralyzed by no known trauma of nerve or sinew; to shake loose the delusion that one is being watched or persecuted or chosen, or the strange sensation that one's body is dissolving or decomposing or that one's sex is changing as he watches helplessly or that one's ability to reach out to others by speech or glance or even touch decays until he stands alone in catatonic stupor, despairing of repair and murderously angry in his silence – all these, and many others that need not be tallied here, are the common province of the psychotherapeutic arts. And the goal of therapy in every case is to restore control of the disordered behaviour to the patient or to eliminate it from the repertory of his behaviours by exerting a complex series of controls over him so that, either way, he will not be troubled by it any more.'[8]

In addition to control by rewards, control may also be exercised by punishment and the infliction of pain, and this also has had a

[8] London, P., *op. cit.*, pp. 42 f.

long history. In this century the technique to gain the most publicity has been electric shock treatment, though since 1950, with the advent of sophisticated drugs, it has been largely replaced. In any case, the aim of such treatment was *not* to inflict pain but to bring relief from overwhelming depression. Today such treatment is given without pain. Since 1950 mood-controlling drugs have become the most commonly used treatment for psychological disabilities of all kinds.

A further method of exercising coercive control – neither so well known nor so developed – is the electrical stimulation of the brain by means of implanted electrodes. For those interested in the details, a recent review is available written by one of the leading investigators in the field, Dr José M. R. Delgado, in the book entitled *The Physical Control of the Mind*.[9] It is clear that not only motor responses, such as flexing or withdrawing a limb, but also changes in feeling the experience of pain or pleasure, can be manipulated by such methods. Once again this is not new in principle but in its degree of scientific sophistication. It must be realized that biological assaults of one sort or another of man upon man have a long history. For example, there was the practice in the ancient world of the castration of males, who as eunuchs could then take charge of harems. What is new is the detailed knowledge and fineness of control made possible by recent advances.

All this adds up to an inescapable challenge. How can man ensure that all this knowledge of behaviour control and manipulation by schedules of reinforcement, by psychoactive drugs and by electrical stimulation of the brain is used to benefit and elevate man and not to degrade and destroy him? The problem of the ethical and moral use of scientific knowledge, whether of nuclear fission or of behaviour control technology, is essentially the same and is not a problem peculiar to Christians. Humanists and all men of good will face it as well, although in a sense, no doubt, it is more acute for the Christian because of his assessment of man as made in the image of God.

    [9] Delgado, J. M. R., *The Physical Control of the Mind* (Harper and Row, New York, 1969).

1

Behaviour therapy

There is one application of our knowledge of behaviour control and modification which raises particular problems for clinical psychologists in their training and professional practice. It concerns the theory and practice of behaviour therapy.

In recent years psychologists have discovered how the judicious application of Skinner's principles of operant conditioning can provide another approach to the treatment of some forms of neurotic illness and to such difficult and hitherto, at times, seemingly intractable problems as homosexuality and chronic alcoholism.

The basic assumption underlying behaviour therapy is that we may usefully regard a variety of conditions including neurotic anxiety, compulsive behaviour, homosexual activity and un-controlled drinking, as examples of inappropriate behaviour which can be modified, shaped, and where necessary eliminated, by the application of operant conditioning and related techniques. Undesirable responses can be extinguished and desirable responses evoked and strengthened.

Those who oppose such methods of behaviour modification often do so on the grounds that the techniques employed are inhuman and simply use mechanical procedures to manipulate people as things. But what in fact happens is frequently the very converse of this. Consider the problem of the chronic alcoholic. The behaviour therapist treats the person concerned as a normal person with a problem he has failed to solve unaided. The patient's responsibility is stressed throughout the course of therapy and his active participation mobilized as much as possible at all times. As one writer, discussing chronic alcoholism as an example of such problems, put it recently,

'It is emphasized that the treatment cannot do the job alone, but it can be expected in most cases to bring the patient's drinking behaviour under his own control. This means that ultimately the patient's self-control will be decisive. In other words, the goal of treatment is to extend that patient's area of freedom of choice to include his drinking behaviour. The patient is also given a realistic appreciation of the chances of success on which to base his decision whether or not to accept the temporary discomforts of treatment. The patient is thus an active participant from the start. He makes the decision to undergo treatment (the nature of which is understood by him), and he plays a decisive role in determining the outcome of treatment. If the treatment succeeds, it releases the patient from his previous slavery to his addiction. In so doing, as the patient usually recognizes himself, it makes him more truly human.'[1]

Some reject the use of aversive stimulation on the grounds that it involves 'punishment'. But a careful scrutiny of what is meant technically by aversive stimulation shows that it has little in common with punishment in the ordinary non-technical sense. Thus Lovibond, in the paper already referred to, points out that,

'In the first place, unlike mere punishment, aversion therapy is not inflicted on an unwilling recipient. Secondly, aversion therapy is not a penalty, because, from the point of view of the behaviour therapist, no offence has been committed. It follows that there can be no retributive or chastening aspects to aversion therapy. The only function which aversion therapy shares with punishment is that of behaviour modification. Apart from obvious technical differences, the modification sought by the behaviour therapist differs fundamentally from the modification usually sought by the punisher.'

And he concludes,

'Hence, both ethical and practical considerations require that aversion therapy be used only when the patient desires to modify his own behaviour, and participates willingly in a programme designed to make it possible for him to do so. Far from being degrading, to the extent that it is successful, such a programme enhances the self-respect of the individual.'

[1] Lovibond, S. H., 'The Ethics of Behaviour Modification' in *The Australian Psychologist,* Vol. 6, No. 3, 1971, pp. 172–180.

Particular ethical problems arise in considering instances where there seem to be grounds for attempting to modify a patient's behaviour without his consent. For example, should one permit the continuance of self-destructive behaviour in a severely retarded child if there are good grounds for believing that the application of behaviour therapy techniques can eliminate such behaviour? The answer, in so far as it allows the child to become more truly human and in control of himself, is surely that behaviour modification should be attempted. It is difficult to formulate guidelines, let alone a rule, but Lovibond boldly attempts to face the issue and concludes as follows:

'Perhaps the general rule should run like this: Manipulation of behaviour without the consent of the individual can be justified only in the case of individuals lacking normal responsibility, and only if the manipulation is designed to move the individual in the direction of rational self-control of behaviour.'

This issue is being actively debated by practising psychologists at the present time. The reason it is raised here is to suggest that there do not seem to be any specifically Christian grounds for opposing the ethical use of such new therapeutic techniques. Indeed, it needs to be said that any technique, as a technique, is ethically neutral, and any method, whether depth therapy based upon psychoanalytic theory, or behaviour therapy, can be applied in an inhuman way. Depth therapy can be used to assault the mind just as effectively, and some would contend with more lasting consequences, as any alleged physical assaults used in aversive stimulation by behaviour therapists. So once again it is not very meaningful to say, Is this or that psychological technique Christian or non-Christian? Ethically it is neutral; but it may be used by good men or bad men, to benefit or to degrade their fellow men.

A Christian assessment
Any Christian assessment of the lines of research just outlined must be influenced by the fact that, as the accelerating pace of

research in the neuro-sciences and in medicine adds to our understanding of the structure and function of the brain, it also holds out high hopes that, with further advances, some of the suffering at present experienced by so much of mankind because of brain dysfunction will slowly give way to therapeutic measures which will relieve this suffering. The research worker who is a Christian will see this as added motivation for him to fulfil, with renewed vigour, his commission 'to subdue the created order' (see Genesis 1:28) so that mankind may benefit from that which God has given us in creation. Men of many other religions, and humanists also, acting from different presuppositions but all motivated by the same concern for the well-being of mankind, will be able to share in this endeavour. Thus our knowledge of the detrimental effects of things like impoverished environment, stress and anxiety, for example, should increase the efforts of those concerned to bring about more widespread acceptance of positive attitudes. Such attitudes will in turn relieve suffering and avoid permanent injury to the brain which would otherwise be reflected in personalities which are cramped and stunted, or deviant in various ways. Perhaps the most obvious and glaring example of an issue on which immediate action could be taken is that of malnutrition. There is now abundant evidence that some forms of malnutrition, especially in small children, result in changes to the structure and biochemistry of the brain which, if they occur at a critical period, may well be irreversible. The net result is the prospect of millions growing up with mental capacities and personality resources less than they could have been had the right kind of food been made available at the right time.

As regards problems which arise concerning the manipulation of behaviour, some scientists, notably Professor B. F. Skinner, have pointed out that already the knowledge that we have of the relation between brain and behaviour is sufficient to present a danger, in that the rapid development of new techniques in the control of behaviour may quickly outstrip the counter controls, which in most countries at the moment prevent exploitation of individuals and groups by the use of force and deception. Despite objections, there is no doubt that science will increasingly facilitate the control of human behaviour and it must be used wisely if we are to avoid disaster.

In spite of the massive increase in research in psycho-pharmacology, examples of which were cited earlier, it seems at present that there is little likelihood of the deliberate wide-scale use of any of the known psychoactive drugs for the control of behaviour of normal people. It is true that there have been many suggestions that drugs have been employed extensively in brain-washing procedures in communist-controlled countries. It is fair to say, however, that, from the reliable evidence available at the present time, this does not seem to be so. Where coercion of persons for the purposes of extracting confession is required, it would seem that the methods employed are police state practices which have been used in various forms since the time of Napoleon. As regards the psychosurgical procedures mentioned earlier, some of which may bring distinct benefit to certain individuals, it is difficult to see how any practical application of them in the future could enable men deliberately to control each other's behaviour in any socially significant way on a large scale.

One other field of neuro-scientific research which we have not had time to comment on in any detail is the study of learning and memory and their relationship to the structure of the brain. It may well be that, in the not too distant future, some of these studies will have practical applications in education and by the same token will be available for exploitation of the public by propagandists.

Finally, a note of warning needs perhaps to be sounded. In this chapter we have indicated some of the ways in which the personality of man is dependent upon the physical structure of the brain including its biochemistry. Such knowledge more fully developed could obviously be abused and become an extremely powerful weapon in the hands of any group who wished to use it, not for the betterment of mankind, but rather to subjugate another group to fulfil their will and purposes. This should surely under-line the necessity for Christians, humanists, men of other religions and all men of good will, to ensure that high principles and clearly-held ethical standards predominate in the affairs of men at all levels, including the application of increasing knowledge in the neuro-sciences.

In addition to such general questions of the ethical use of knowledge of behaviour-control technology just discussed, certain more specific questions arise for the Christian. For instance, some might argue thus: 'The capacity for "being anxious for nothing" is a consequence, according to Scripture, of a deep trust in a sovereign Lord, whose love is unchanging and care unlimited. But now the behaviour technologist tells us that he can readily enable us to be "anxious for nothing" by the judicious use of an appropriate psychoactive drug. What then of faith and trust?' Or again, someone may say: 'The fruit of the Spirit includes gentleness, kindness, long suffering; but if we are genetically endowed with a somewhat aggressive personality, these are difficult to experience and show. Moreover, we now know how aggressive behaviour can be turned on and off by the electrical stimulation of certain brain structures. Why then dedicate oneself to showing gentleness, kindness and long suffering when a suitable application of behaviour technology techniques can produce instant behaviour changes to order?'

Such issues are not just hypothetical. Most readers will know (or know of) a relative, friend, or acquaintance who has suffered from an acute anxiety state or an episode of depression. They may have had such experiences themselves. They will also know how frequently such states have been relieved by appropriate medication with psychoactive drugs. Such knowledge leads some to ask, 'Why did my faith not work? I did not want to be anxious, I did try to trust and "be anxious for nothing" but it did not work.'

These are difficult questions indeed. A clue to the answers comes from distinguishing between normal anxiety and depression – the lot of all mankind – and abnormal anxiety states and depressive illnesses. Whilst no clear, hard and fast distinction can easily be made, it needs to be remembered that scriptural statements are in general addressed to the common lot of all mankind. It also helps to draw the analogy here between mental and physical illnesses. People with acute anxiety states or severe depressions are sick people and need help and healing. In the cases of physical illnesses God expects us to seek healing through the use, with thanksgiving, of the knowledge he has given us through medical science. Likewise in the case of many psychological illnesses, which may well have a physical basis, we should with thankfulness apply similar God-given resources in the form of psychoactive drugs and a variety of psychotherapeutic procedures. It is also essential to remember that the Bible does not teach that Christians will escape hardship and suffering. Rather it teaches that, although suffering is the common lot of all men, the Christian can find in Christ the resources to endure such sufferings with fortitude and without resentment. For Christ himself has lived as a man; 'he himself has passed through the test of suffering' (Hebrews 2:18) and ' . . . because of his likeness to us, has been tested every way, only without sin' (Hebrews 4:15).

What some find difficult to accept is that, just as we all have propensities or tendencies by reason of our physical make-up which make it more or less likely that we shall develop certain forms of physical illness and not others, so, being psychosomatic unities, we also have greater or lesser proneness to develop certain kinds of mental illness. This topic of the physical basis of mental states is an extremely complex and difficult one, fraught with problems even for those well acquainted with the field. But such preliminary clues as we have from studies of, for example, individual differences in conditioning rates, in emotional responses and in physical responses to environmental stresses, indicate a close linkage between physical make-up and psychological processes. Other evidence comes from studies linking changes in body biochemistry with certain kinds of mental illness. This is not new. For long we have been aware of the mental strains which many women undergo at certain stages of their menopause and, indeed, of their normal menstrual cycle. What is new is the increasing precision we are developing for linking physical with mental changes.

As regards the second issue raised above concerning the use of behaviour-technology to generate some of the fruit of the Spirit, it must be remembered that man's standards of assessment are not God's. For 'man looks on the outward appearance [the behaviour], but the Lord looks on the heart' (1 Samuel 16:7 RSV) and 'My thoughts are not your thoughts . . . For as the heavens are higher than the earth, so are ... my thoughts than your thoughts' (Isaiah 55:8, 9).

Let me enlarge on this. By way of illustration let us imagine a situation in which we have the opportunity to observe closely two men in their professional and personal lives. One is the son of an evangelical bishop, brought up in a Christian home, schooled at a Christian school and trained to accept and practise a high ethical and moral code. On leaving home he thinks a great deal about his faith, and finally decides he cannot any longer believe in the divinity of Christ and severs all formal connections with Christian groups. The other man was brought up by an alcoholic father and a mother who thought nothing of being unfaithful to her dissolute husband. He was maltreated, taught the ways of deceit, lying and stealing, and how to practise them with material profit to himself. At the age of twenty-eight he is converted quite suddenly at an evangelistic meeting. A process of learning, of Christian discipleship, begins, but his habitual ways of behaving die hard as he slowly sees and applies the implications of his new-found faith to every aspect of his life. Ethically and morally he still has lapses into his old ways, so that from an observer's viewpoint he behaves less in conformity with Christian principles than the avowedly non-Christian son of the evangelical bishop. In one sense, some of the behavioural aspects of the fruit of the Spirit are more evident in the life of the non-Christian than the Christian. It would be quite erroneous, however, to question therefore the reality of Christian conversion. What is striking is the contrast between what he is, and what he is becoming, with what he recently was. On that criterion, he bears a striking testimony as compared with his Christ-denying, ethical, moral and pleasant contemporary. The point is a simple one. We can easily fall into the trap of ignoring or denying our individuality, our genetic endowment, the built-in effects of our upbringing and, in so doing, we effectively make a non-Christian assessment of ourselves and of others.

In all discussion of this kind it is vitally important to remember that, as Christians, we believe that God alone knows how he has made each one of us. We are taught that those to whom much has been given, from them will much be required, but that 'he knows how we were made, he knows full well that we are dust' (Psalm 103:14).

7 Men, machines and moral choices

The question is often posed, 'Is it not the case that all the accumulating evidence from the biological and behavioural sciences points more and more to the conclusion that man's belief in freedom of choice and freedom of action is nothing more than a comforting illusion?' If the answer to this question is 'Yes', then clearly that has far-reaching implications for Christian beliefs since, if a man has no freedom of choice, we must ask in what sense he can be held responsible for his acceptance or rejection of the claims of Christ. Or again, if he has no freedom of action, in what sense can he be held morally culpable for behaviour which breaks God's revealed laws? We shall consider each of these issues in turn. As we do so we hope that our approach will suggest constructive ways of examining other similar problems, not dealt with here, but which have arisen, or might well arise, with new developments in psychology and other behavioural sciences.

Determinism: the background

It is easy to sympathize with a psychology student who develops the impression that freedom of choice may, after all, be only an illusion. In course after course he learns about the determinants of behaviour. These include the effects of early experience, of group pressures, of physiological and biochemical factors, of genetically blue-printed brain structure and so on. Add to all these the assumption which we have earlier described as 'methodological determinism', implicit in the whole approach of psychology today, and what begins as a vague impression may soon become a very uncomfortable feeling of loss of personal autonomy.

The first thing to realize is that determinism is not a new problem, thought up by psychologists, but one which has been discussed by philosophers for many centuries. In the last fifty years, however, it has become very much more acute. This has been due to the rapid growth in the behavioural sciences where the emerging picture of the lawfulness of behaviour has given encouragement to the determinist presuppositions held by some philosophers and psychologists. It is important, at this stage, to realize that this is not a problem just for Christians. All who believe that man has choice and carries responsibility are confronted with it. Christians, however, are particularly concerned because of their belief that choices made now have extremely important implications, not only for the whole of this life, but also for the life beyond. They are faced with passages of Scripture which demand a decision. Christ invites a man to 'come' to him (Matthew 11:28), or to 'receive' him (John 1:12). Time and again the choice is given to come or not to come, to follow or not to follow, to receive or not to receive, to believe or not to believe. There is, therefore, an inescapable thread of teaching that man is continually confronted with choices which he must face, decisions for which he is personally responsible.

Another point to which we shall refer again later is that the problem has recently become much more acute because of our own efforts as behavioural and neuro-scientists. Our most favoured scientific models of the workings of the brain incorporate a large element of physical determinism. This inevitably has raised, with a fresh urgency, the rethinking of traditional beliefs about freedom of choice and action. As we indicated earlier, those of us who work as psychologists assume some form of determinism, otherwise we could not even get started on our research; some of us adopt what is called a 'strong' form of determinism, and others merely a 'weak' form, the latter being a form of determinism within statistical limits only.

Before we get down to the details, however, it is worth noting that it is very easy to become so preoccupied with the problem of determinism that our judgment becomes distorted to such an extent that we lose sight of the most obvious thing of all. This is that *the experience and the awareness of freedom of choice and action is common to the vast majority of men in all ages. It is just not possible to ignore this.* It is, if you like, another aspect of the inter-subjective verifiability which, as Michael Polanyi has shown, is so basic to the scientific enterprise itself. So common an experience as freedom of choice cannot be lightly laid aside on the basis of a particular, current, scientific model of brain functioning, because to do that would be simply to sweep the most immediate evidence under the carpet.

Finally let me say that I have considerable sympathy with those who feel that too many are writing on this subject today because it is fashionable to do so. Some would even say it is no more than tilting at a windmill. For many, however, it is a very real and formidable windmill and for that reason alone we must take a look at it now.

Defining the problem

The issue in simple terms boils down to the question whether we enjoy any real freedom of choice or whether all of our actions are inevitable and unavoidable. In other words, is our experience of freedom and choice an illusion? No-one of course is denying that we all act in character most of the time. We are all aware of the way in which we ourselves and our friends act extremely predictably in most situations. Certainly our actions are predictable to those who know us well. For behavioural scientists the problem emerges most clearly when studying the relation between brain processes and behaviour. In its extreme form it is sometimes posed as follows: 'If my brain is a physically determinate system, then in what sense can I be said to have any freedom of choice?'

For the benefit of the non-psychologists who are reading this, we should point out that today most university courses in psychology include a course of lectures on the biological bases of behaviour. Psychology students are required to know something of the structure and function of the brain and the central nervous system. The intention of such courses is that the students should begin to understand the ways in which psychological processes such as learning, perceiving and remembering are dependent for their normal functioning upon the intactness of the central nervous system. Whilst this is not the place to attempt to give a miniature course in neuro-psychology, nevertheless a few simple examples should perhaps be given. The non-specialist reader will then have some idea of the kinds of experimental findings whose implications Christian students often feel generate problems regarding the nature of man particularly in the realm of moral responsibility.

Let us take first an example of psychosurgery of the kind which has been much debated in public recently. Damage to, or removal of, certain parts of the frontal area of the brain can modify behaviour in such a way that a person who previously might have been ambitious, well adjusted and highly motivated will lose his former drive, become insensitive to the feeling of others, disorganized and tactless, and may manifest a general lack of responsiveness to ethical and moral considerations. Not infrequently such persons also report a general feeling of euphoria. Surgical intervention of this kind was, at one time, widely used with some psychiatric patients who failed to get relief by any other means.

Another example that may be cited is the effect of removal of, or damage to, certain parts of the temporal lobe. In such cases there may follow difficulty in remembering recent events or, more seriously, changes in emotional responsiveness. Appropriately placed lesions of this kind may increase aggressiveness or may decrease it; may increase the strength of the sexual drive or may reduce it. The details are not important here. They are mentioned to indicate how changes in feeling and behaviour can be brought about by appropriate modifications to the structure of the brain.

What is true of such gross changes is also true at a more molecular level. It is now clear that changes in the biochemistry of the brain may produce dramatic changes in how a person feels and behaves. One of the most intensive areas of research in physiological psychology today is the study of brain chemistry and behaviour. The best-known examples of this are, of course, the extremely widespread use of a whole range of tranquillizing drugs. It need hardly be emphasized that, in one sense, there is nothing terribly new in this since for a very long time the existence of so-called psychotropic drugs has been well documented in the history of the human race. What is new is that the mode of action of these drugs is becoming more clearly understood. As a result, the possibility of their widespread abuse becomes a matter of serious concern.

Current research into the effects of the early physical and social environment also has implications of a moral kind. Both of these can apparently produce irreversible changes in the structure and function of the nervous system. This in turn places limits upon the behaviour of which the organism is capable in adulthood. It has been shown, for example, that in animals impoverished environments in early life can produce irreversible changes in brain chemistry. These, in turn, are accompanied by stunted behaviour and limitations on learning capacity in later life. Once again, the details of this are not important here but the moral implications are. We may note in passing that this evidence, and there is a great deal of it available now, underlines very clearly one of the points made earlier, namely that man is a psychosomatic or psychophysical unity.

To illustrate this latter point, consider a problem in which ethical and moral issues arise and in which the influence of these two variables, the biological and the environmental, upon behaviour are both known to be important. I refer to juvenile delinquency. Whatever particular classification is used of the different forms of juvenile delinquency, it tends to reflect the emphasis given to the biological and environmental factors respectively. In the past the greater part of research into the causes of delinquency has focused upon the environmental factors. More recent reports have emphasized the intrinsic, that is the factors which are biologically based. For example, a recent report reads as follows:

'The relative contribution of hereditary and environmental factors to the causation of adult criminality remains an open question. The preponderance of opinion favours the greater importance of social and environmental factors in determining whether an individual falls into criminality or he does not; but the type of crime into which he may drift, and the extent to which his life is governed by criminal tendencies, would seem to be largely a reflection of his personality, with genetic factors lending much that is most characteristic.'[1]

Early studies of delinquency certainly laid great emphasis on poverty, over-crowding and economic disadvantages of the homes from which delinquents came. Added to this were the effects of others in the home, disturbed family life, broken homes and educational deprivation. As many workers have pointed out, however, correlates of delinquency are not necessarily causes and, as one recent example shows, using unusually representative and satisfactory sampling techniques, there is now a shift towards the middle social class of the Registrar General's classification.

More recently, along with our rapidly increasing knowledge of genetics, there has been a renewed interest in physiological causal factors of delinquency. Here there are broadly two different kinds of theories – those genetic theories that make physical factors directly causative of delinquency, and those where the connection is less straightforward. The latter argue for a predisposition to delinquent behaviour which then develops under certain circumstances. The strongly and directly causative view of genetic factors is not consistently supported, and what emerges is a view of physical factors as predisposing, *via* temperamental traits, to delinquent behaviour in association with other factors such as social ones. The effect of such theories is to focus attention upon the criminal rather than upon the legal system or upon social environmental factors.

Once again, our intention is not to go into an extremely complicated problem but merely to point out that, in an issue of this kind, one cannot ignore as determinants of behaviour intrinsic factors of a physiological and genetic kind. But such knowledge

[1] Cowie, J., Cowie, V., Slater, R., *Delinquency in Girls* (Heinemann, London, 1968), p. 174.

raises with fresh urgency questions concerning a person's moral responsibility for his actions. After this somewhat lengthy digression we must now return to our main discussion.

It is not only the physiological psychologists who have been confronted with this problem of freedom and choice. There are others who would pose the same question but at a different level, particularly if they have been strongly influenced by the work of Professor Skinner. In the context of his kind of approach to the study of behaviour the question would be phrased as:

'If my behaviour is determined by contingencies of reinforcement then in what sense can I be held responsible for my present behaviour patterns, since all are determined and predictable from past experience?'

Not surprisingly we find Skinner saying in some of his writings,

'If we are to use the methods of science in the field of human affairs we must assume that behaviour is lawful and determined.'

In addition, we find a similar view expressed by other psychologists whose approach is much more psychodynamic. An example here would be Professor Carl Rogers, who has written,

'Behaviour, when it is examined scientifically, is surely best understood as determined by prior causation. This is one great fact of science.'

(In passing one may, perhaps, take Professor Rogers to task for confusing what he calls 'one great fact of science' with what is really an assumption of scientists.)

A little thought soon reveals that such views as those expressed by Skinner and Rogers have strange implications for Skinner and Rogers themselves. For example, does Skinner's view mean that he had no freedom to arrive at any conclusion other than the one he expressed in the quotation just given? According to his own formulation, was his own verbalization no more than the determinate outcome of the schedules of reinforcement to which Skinner's life events had exposed him over the years? Or, again, are there any external criteria, on Skinner's view, for deciding whether or not Skinner himself is right or wrong? Or are words like 'right/wrong', 'true/untrue' not legitimate on his view?

In a recent book Sir Norman Anderson has raised the same paradox in another context. When discussing morality and determinism he has written,

'But this [determinism] is a philosophy of life which it is very difficult, to say the least, to maintain consistently and to defend convincingly in practice. A friend of mine who is a convinced determinist, for example, has written an excellent little book on how students should set out on the study of the subject he professes so ably (what habits and attitudes of mind they should seek to develop, how they should learn to use a library, what sort of notes they should make, etc.). Elsewhere, however, he tells us that "on a determinist view every impulse, if in fact not resisted, was in those circumstances irresistible. A so-called irresistible impulse is simply one in which the desire to perform a particular act is not influenced by other factors." Thus the only justification for promulgating criminal laws, for example, is that "for mankind in the mass it is impossible to tell whom the threat of punishment will restrain and whom it will not. For most it will succeed; for some it will fail, and the punishment must then be applied to these criminals in order to maintain the threat for persons generally." So we must, presumably, conclude that it was because of an irresistible impulse that he wrote his book; that the existence of this book, and the admirable advice it contains, must be regarded as one factor in evoking in some students an irresistible impulse to study effectively, although in other cases it will inevitably fail in its purpose; and that the students concerned have no real liberty of choice whether to be industrious or idle, systematic or slipshod – or, indeed, whether to choose to read this book at all, should circumstances, or some well-meaning friend, ever bring it to their attention.'[2]

In other words it seems very difficult to reconcile an extreme mechanistic-determinist view with the exercise of rational thought. If the workings of every man's mind are exclusively determined by the mechanics of the brain, then how can it be shown that one man's view is correct and another's mistaken? How indeed can the most convinced determinist defend his philosophy of life? In J. B. S. Haldane's words, quoted by Professor Anderson,

'If my mental processes are determined wholly by the motions of the atoms in my brain, I have no reason to suppose that my beliefs are true . . . and hence I have no reason for supposing my brain to be composed of atoms.'

Professor Carl Rogers, referred to above, has his own solution to this self-generated problem. It is

'that responsible personal choice, which is the core experience of psychotherapy, and which exists prior to any scientific endeavour, is an equally prominent fact in our lives. To deny the experience of responsible choice is as restricted a view as to deny the possibility of behavioural science.'

In fact this is Professor Rogers' way of referring to the inter-subjective verifiability mentioned above. Many prominent physiologists share his view. For example, the Nobel Prize Winner in Medicine, Professor Sir J. C. Eccles has written in these terms.[3]

Proposed solutions to the problem

A number of different solutions have been proposed. First, there are those which, whilst conceding that the body is a physically

[2] Anderson, J. N. D., *Morality, Law and Grace* (Tyndale Press, London, 1972), pp. 10–11, quoting G. L. Williams, *The Criminal Law* (Stevens, London, 1953), pp. 346 f.

[3] Eccles, J. C., ed., *Brain and Conscious Experience* (Springer-Verlag, New York, 1966).

determinate stuff, maintain that mind is not bound to the body but enjoys a certain autonomy of its own. Such views are often, though not exclusively, held by those with interests in subjects such as para-psychology, extra-sensory perception, psychical research, and so on. It is indeed a defensible view, and in 1950 Laslett edited a book entitled *The Physical Basis of Mind*[4] in which a number of extremely distinguished biological scientists reached something approaching a consensus of opinion to the effect that the neural activity of the brain somehow *interacts* with the private world of the mind. The question arises, however, is it necessary to hold a dualist view in order to safeguard man's freedom?

Another form of dualism which has been canvassed in the past might be labelled 'dualism of descriptive categories'. On this view freedom and determinism are concepts belonging to two different language systems. Its advocates argue that both are necessary to do justice to our present scientific knowledge and to the experience of human freedom. Thus, for example, Neil Bohr speaks of freedom and determinism as complementary descriptions, drawing attention to the analogy of wave-particle models in physics. Amongst psychologists, Professor Rogers, referred to above, takes a similar view. Certainly this view avoids some of the difficulties of the dualism of stuff approach. Yet others simply point out that, whilst determinism is a useful postulate *within science*, that does not mean that it is a universal rule about the world. It is one thing, they argue, to employ it as a useful rule of procedure for scientific enquiry, yet another to go on to assert that such a rule expresses an intrinsic property of the created order.

Yet another form has been advocated by some distinguished scientists who, having accepted the force of the scientific evidence, see a clue to the solution to the problem within science itself. Their appeal is to a particular scientific principle, namely the Heisenberg principle of indeterminacy in physics. The best-known champion of such a view has been Sir John Eccles, referred to above. On his view the main features of the situation are as follows. First, that some form of mind/brain liaison occurs in the

[4] Laslett, P., ed., *The Physical Basis of Mind* (Macmillan, London, 1950).

cortex (that is, in the large convoluted surface of the brain's cerebral hemispheres). The will, it is asserted, can influence neural activity without violating physical laws because the energy involved in such influence is within the limits of the Heisenberg uncertainty principle.

In the simplest possible terms the Heisenberg principle states that, where there are certain pairs of variables which specify what is happening at the level of the interactions of the smallest known particles, such as electrons, we find that there are peculiar relationships operating, and that the more accurately one of the quantities is known, the less accurately is the other quantity predictable. For example, the more accurately the position of an electron is measured in an experimental set-up, the greater is the uncertainty in any prediction about its velocity. The errors of measurement, therefore, that come in under these circumstances are not the ordinary type of error that can be reduced by improving the sensitivity of the apparatus; they are, so it is asserted, inherent in the structure of matter.

When this is applied to our present problem the picture which emerges is of neural activity being influenced by non-physical factors. Thus Eccles believes that mind, being one such non-physical factor, either may influence individual quantum events, these effects then being amplified throughout the cortex, or, more probably, there could be a co-ordinated shifting of probabilities in many such events simultaneously.

We may make a number of comments on Eccles' view. First of all, the indeterminacy allowed by the Heisenberg principle becomes more and more negligible the bigger the objects that we are studying. Whilst for the study of electrons it is far from negligible, nevertheless, by the time we get to the size of the neuron, which is a million million million times heavier than an electron, it is already becoming negligible. Second, the brain, as far as we can see at the moment, seems to be organized on a team-work basis so that one brain cell behaving unpredictably would make no significant difference to the over-all functioning of the brain. Third, the random fluctuations in the brain attributable to Heisenberg's principle are extremely small compared with other fluctuations known to us, such as those due to thermodynamic changes, to random fluctuations in the blood supply, and so on. In fact, what we must conclude here is that such unpredictable disturbances could as easily be used to excuse me from responsibility as to credit me with responsibility for my choices.

There is one aspect of this latter view which we might label as 'modified dualism', which is extremely vulnerable to further scientific advances if we are to take seriously the opinions of some very distinguished scientists such as Einstein and Bohm. They have contended that the Heisenberg indeterminacy principle is simply an expression of our present ignorance in this field of science. Whilst Neil Bohr was convinced that uncertainty is not a product of our ignorance, but a fundamental limitation on our human knowledge permanently preventing us from knowing whether certain events are determinate or not, his view is not shared by Einstein and Bohm. The reader may well feel, as does the writer, Who, then, are we to decide? But perhaps we can push the question one stage further back, and ask, Do we need to pin our defence of freedom on the Heisenberg uncertainty principle? That is the question that we must turn to now, and the answer given in the next section suggests that we do not.

'Logical indeterminacy' and freedom of choice

Since Professor Donald MacKay's views on determinism and brain science have been widely publicized in recent years they will not be dealt with here in detail. I shall concentrate simply on the specific question of why, on MacKay's view, a deterministic model of the physical working of the brain would not render untenable the belief that under normal circumstances a man enjoys freedom of choice and action.

Many people have found MacKay's views difficult to follow, particularly on first meeting them. In order to help overcome some of that difficulty I shall try to illustrate his argument with a series of diagrams.

First, we must ask, What does MacKay mean by 'free to choose'? Quoting from a recent publication[5] of MacKay's we may answer,

---

[5] MacKay, D. M., *The Clockwork Image* (IVP, London, 1974), p. 110.

'by calling a man "free", (a) we might mean that his action was *unpredictable by anyone*. This I would call the freedom of caprice; *or* (b) we may mean that the outcome of his decision is *up to him*, in the sense that unless he makes the decision it will not be made, that he is in a position to make it, and that no fully-determinate specification of the outcome already exists, which he would be correct to accept as inevitable, and would be unable to falsify, if only he knew it.'

Secondly, how much exemption from deterministic physical laws does MacKay have to assume for the brain? His argument would hold good even if the machinery of our brains were as physically determinate as the solar system, and he makes no appeal to Heisenberg's uncertainty principle in order to reconcile mechanistic ideas of the brain with freedom of choice.

Third, how much independence does MacKay have to postulate between a man's thoughts and beliefs and the physical state of his brain? None. He considers for the sake of argument the assumption that *all* that a person experiences (sees, feels, believes, thinks) is in some precise way represented in the physical state of his brain, and shows that even this extreme assumption would not be incompatible with human freedom in sense (b) above.

Now that the main assumptions under consideration are clear let me try to illustrate MacKay's argument with some diagrams.

If a man's brain is in State A, his beliefs (thoughts and knowledge) corresponding to that brain state may be represented as **a** (see fig. 1).

If the man's beliefs change from **a** to **b**, then his physical brain state must change from A to B. This follows from the assumption that what a man believes, thinks, knows, *etc.*, cannot be disconnected from the 'cognitive machinery' of his brain. This is rather like saying that when the advertisement on a TV screen changes from a pattern which we read as DRINK MORE MILK, to one which we read as EAT MORE MEAT, there must be a changed pattern of blobs to carry with it the changed message and meaning.

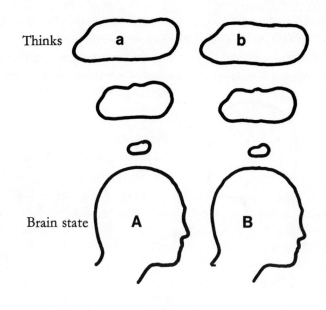

Fig. 1

MacKay is not himself concerned either to advocate or oppose this assumption. He merely asks:

'what would follow *if* all our mental activity *were* rigorously represented by some activity of our brain mechanism, so that no change could take place in what we perceived, thought, believed, *etc.*, without some corresponding change taking place in the state of that mechanism?'[6]

To see what *would* follow, let us set up a hypothetical situation (fig. 2) in which we, as brain scientists, are prepared to predict the

[6] MacKay, D. M., 'The Bankruptcy of Determinism' in *The New Scientist*, 2 July 1970, pp. 24–26.

behaviour of Mr. X from our knowledge of his brain state. We have assessed his brain state as being A. On the basis of this we confidently deduce what his next move (say a word or action) will be. Thus brain state A leads us to make a prediction PA.

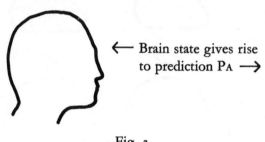

← Brain state gives rise
to prediction PA →

Fig. 2

Now, if we are good brain scientists we can sit back and wait patiently to see our prediction PA fulfilled. Moreover, we can offer our prediction PA to anyone standing by (so long as A is unaffected) and let the bystander see how good we are at predicting.

But now let us ask: is our prediction PA something that Mr X himself would be correct to believe, if only he knew it?

To answer, we must see what difference it would make to Mr X's brain if he *were* to believe PA. If his believing PA would change his brain from state A to state B, then if he believed PA his brain would no longer be in the state (A) on which we based our prediction PA. Using our diagrams, we can see how the state of affairs would change. Note that the new brain state B would then give rise to a new prediction PB (see fig. 3).

But, it may be asked, could we not, as experts in brain science, allow for the effects of offering our prediction to X, and thus make prediction PB? We could indeed: but if we did we should then be *wrong* to claim that prediction PB is what Mr X would be correct

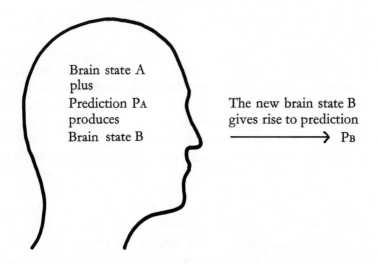

Brain state A
plus
Prediction Pa
produces
Brain state B

The new brain state B
gives rise to prediction

$\longrightarrow$ Pb

Fig. 3.   The effect of feeding prediction Pa into brain state A

to believe, because, as we have already agreed, it is brain state B
that leads to prediction Pb. But if Mr X believed prediction Pb,
his brain would be changed into still another state, C, to which
Pb would not apply.

It turns out then that our prediction Pa is a valid one for *us*
providing we keep quiet about it to the man about whom it is
made. Put another way, our prediction is a conditional one, in the
sense that it is correct *only* on condition that it is not believed by
the person it concerns most intimately. To call it a 'true' prediction
is, therefore, a strange use of the word 'true'. Normally, if something is true, it is true for everyone; but this prediction is not like
that, for it is something Mr X would be *mistaken* to believe.
MacKay refers to the status which this curious relationship
between brain states and cognitive states confers upon our future
actions as 'logical indeterminacy'. It forces us to make a sharp
distinction between calling an action 'predictable' (by onlookers)
and calling it 'inevitable' (for the agent). It shows that in this area

what is correct for onlookers to believe may not be *what is correct* for agents to believe.

To sum up then. As our diagrams have tried to illustrate, whilst if mechanistic assumptions were true we could, in principle, produce a specification of someone's future behaviour, nevertheless such a prediction would have a claim to be believed only by others and *not* by the person concerned. This is another way of saying that 'no fully-determinate specification of the outcome already exists, which he would be correct to accept as inevitable, and would be unable to falsify, if only he knew it'.[7] If he did know the onlookers' prediction he would be *mistaken* to believe it!

Note that this proves much more than that *we cannot know* our own future. What MacKay has shown is that, even on mechanistic assumptions, our future *has no complete specification* with an unconditional claim to our assent until we determine that future by making up our minds.

MacKay sums it up like this:

'To test the strength of the argument, let us take the most favourable case imaginable by the determinist. Suppose that from our observations of Joe's brain and its environment we can write down, well in advance, a whole series of predictions that we keep secret until after the events, and then triumphantly produce to Joe as a proof of our success. By showing him a ciné film of the calculating process, we convince him beyond doubt that our mechanistic theory of his brain is correct. Would not this show at least retrospectively that he was mistaken in believing that he was facing genuinely open possibilities?

'It would not. It would show, of course, that the outcome was *predictable by us*. What it would not show is that it was *inevitable for him*. It cannot do so, for it cannot produce a specification of the outcome that Joe would have been unconditionally correct to accept before he made up his mind. In this sense, no matter how many detached observers could predict the outcome, Joe – and you and I – are free in choosing. We cannot logically escape (or be denied) responsibility for our choices

[7] See above, p. 124.

on the grounds of their predictability by non-participant observers.'[8]

One of the noteworthy features of MacKay's views is that, unlike those of Sperry (see below) and of Eccles, which are different versions of a dualist account postulating *interaction* between the mental and the physical, MacKay's account can be more accurately described as a multi-aspect account of the nature of man and his mental life. He regards man as a unity, of which the physical is one aspect, the mental another, the spiritual yet another. He insists that it is essential, in attempting to do full justice to the mystery of man as man, to take account of each aspect of his functioning. But he argues that in order to do so there is no need to assume two parallel sets of *events*, one mental, the other physical. Rather, he would say, we have one mysterious set of events, rich enough to require accounts of all these different aspects if we are not to miss some of the truth about our human nature and our human actions.

Summing up

We have argued that to hold a dualist position is defensible and may not be regarded as obscurantist on the present evidence. Indeed, it is held by a number of distinguished scientists today. For example, one leading brain scientist, Professor Roger Sperry, himself a very concerned and outspoken humanist, has written as follows:

'Science can see the brain as a complexed electro-chemical communications network full of nerve excitations, all governed by respectable scientific laws of bio-physics, bio-chemistry, and physiology; but few investigators, and none that I know, have been ready to tolerate an injection into this causal machinery of any mental or conscious forces. This, then, in brief, is the general stance of modern science out of which has come today's prevailing objective, mechanistic, materialistic, beha- viouristic, reductionistic, fatalistic, view of the nature of mind

[8] MacKay, D. M., *art. cit.,* p. 25.

and psyche. This kind of thinking is not confined to our laboratories and classrooms, of course. It leaks and spreads, and though never officially imposed on the societies of our western world, we nevertheless see on all sides the pervasive influence of creeping materialism.'[9]

Faced with this situation, Professor Sperry said that he is prepared to align himself with the approximately 0·1% mentalist minority in support of a hypothetical brain model in which consciousness and mental forces generally are given their due representation as important features of the control. These, he said, appear in active operational forces and dynamic properties that interact with and upon the physiological machinery. In effect, Professor Sperry is adopting a dualist and interactionist point of view concerning the relationship between mind and body. Furthermore, he criticizes attempts, as he put it, 'to restore freewill to the human brain, by recourse to various forms of indeterminacy, physical, logical, emergent, or others'. He believes they have failed, so far as he can see, to do much more than introduce, perhaps, a bit of unpredictable caprice into our comportment that most of us would prefer to be without. Professor Sperry's view thus solves the problem of our freedom at a stroke, because for him conscious forces, mind, or whatever you like to call them, are not uniquely tied to the physical embodiment which is the deterministic system.

We have shown that the other view, put forward by Eccles, is also defensible; but we believe it has several flaws, and may well be vulnerable in the long run with the advances of physics.

Finally, we have looked at the way in which MacKay has shown what does and does not follow from assuming that the brain is a physically determinate system and that all that a person experiences (sees, feels, believes, thinks) is in some precise way represented in the physical state of his brain. He discovers that the kind of freedom which goes with responsibility is not endangered by such a model.

But problems remain. Clearly, our present behaviour *is*

⁹ Sperry, R. W., *Bulletin of the Atomic Scientists*, Vol. 22, No. 7, 1966, pp. 2–6.

dependent upon our genetic endowment and upon our early upbringing – the social, cultural and physical environment in which we have grown up. These factors could certainly summate to make it more difficult for some people than others to become and to be Christians. There is nothing in Christianity, however, to deny that men differ and certainly nothing to suggest that a man will be judged for failing to make decisions which, by his very constitution, he could not make.

That having been said, it is well to remember that the crux of being a Christian is not having a full intellectual grasp of a set of theological doctrines; nor is it a matter of coming to God with an attitude of gratitude; nor is it being able to analyse all the factors which make us feel a need to come to terms with him, if he does exist. Rather, in essence, it is exercising, however feebly, however haltingly, however vaguely at first, a capacity that all have grown up with, however much of a battering it may have taken due to the circumstances of our lives, namely the capacity to respond as one person to another. The Christian assertion is that that other person is not an abstract God defined in terms of absolutes, but rather a loving, compassionate, and caring friend, Jesus Christ himself, aptly described in the Gospels as 'the friend of sinners'. It is at this point that one is thankful for the experience of millions who can testify that, in making the smallest move in response to the glimmer of an understanding of such love, they were led on to the awareness that God himself had already moved towards them, and that a loving welcome awaited them. It is in these terms that Christ's invitation 'Come unto me' is as meaningful today as ever it was.

8 Conversion: evaluating the psychological accounts

We have already seen that the majority of psychologists regard their discipline as the science of behaviour. Like other scientists they construct theories and models aimed at producing a coherent account of the data gathered from observation and experiment. Such theories differ from their pre-scientific predecessors mainly in that they are more precise and the terms used in them are operationally defined, referring as they do to observable events. In principle there is thus no reason why the same approach should not be used in the investigation of observable aspects of religious behaviour. Although the psychology of religion has never formed a major part of contemporary psychology there has nevertheless been a steady stream of publications on this topic, including the better known works of James, Freud, Thouless, Allport, Argyle and Mowrer. In addition, there have been other more speculative contributions which have, from time to time, aroused considerable interest, particularly if they have been presented as alternatives to traditional religious explanations of the same behaviour. In this chapter we shall illustrate the kinds of explanation of religious behaviour offered by psychologists by focusing on the, at times, controversial phenomenon of religious conversion.

When an evangelistic crusade is in progress it is not uncommon to hear the criticism made that 'conversion is just emotionalism' or that 'conversion is all psychological'. In a moment we shall examine such assertions in detail paying particular attention to the question of how to relate psychological explanations of conversion with traditional Christian explanations. But first let us elaborate what we mean by psychological accounts of religious conversion.

It is interesting to recall that, in the past, some Christians, understandably attaching great worth to their religious experiences, have felt that religious behaviour is too sacred to be investigated by psychologists, whether believers or unbelievers. Whilst one may sympathize with this view it is difficult to agree with it. Religious behaviour is, after all, so much a part of human life and is so varied that it is potentially a very rewarding field of study for psychologists, especially those interested in cross-cultural studies. No doubt one reason for some apprehension on the part of believers has been the unjustified assertions of some non-Christians that to come up with a possible psychological explanation of religious behaviour is to *explain that behaviour away* and, by implication, to dispose of any necessity to take seriously the beliefs of the person whom they have studied behaving religiously. The fallacy of the reasoning behind such an attitude is amusingly brought out in a story by Professor Allport of the young undergraduate who, after hearing Archbishop William Temple give an address at Oxford, opened up the discussion by commenting, 'Well, of course, Archbishop, the point is that you believe what you believe because of the way you were brought up.' To which, so the report goes, the Archbishop quietly and coolly replied, 'That is as it may be. But the fact remains that you believe that I believe what I believe because of the way I was brought up, because of the way you were brought up.' And that, of course, is simply a polite way of pointing out that that kind of statement is nothing more than the entry to an infinite logical regress. Or put less politely, it is just another example of an amusing pastime which gets one nowhere, namely, of psychological mud-slinging. As a ploy to avoid taking another man's beliefs seriously it is, unfortunately, not uncommon.

Conversion, brain-washing and wishful thinking
A good reason for taking conversion as our example is that, for those who take seriously the words of the founder of the Christian

faith, conversion is not, so to speak, an optional extra for those taking honours in Christianity, something which those just taking a pass degree can avoid; rather it is of the essence of being a Christian. Christ said, 'Except ye be converted, . . . ye shall not enter into the kingdom of heaven' (Matthew 18:3 AV). Since our aim is to consider the relationship of religious and psychological explanations of religious behaviour, we shall not attempt any kind of a comprehensive review of what psychologists have said about conversion. For those who wish to make such a review there is a large professional literature which they may consult. Some psychologists have concentrated on studying the effects of the physical and social environment when conversion occurs. Others have speculated about physiological processes occurring in the brain as a result of the stress involved in some conversions. Psychodynamic processes of the kind that Freud talked about have provided an explanatory framework for other accounts of conversion. We may take any of these psychological explanations and ask, How should it be related to the explanations that traditionally have been given by Christians about the same behaviour?

Three types of explanation
In order to keep our discussion to manageable proportions we shall oversimplify and classify the diversity of explanations into three groups. These we shall label social-learning-type theories, psychophysiological-type theories and psychodynamic-type theories.

1. Social-learning-type theories have emphasized the formative influence of the social and cultural environment on the nature of a person's religious beliefs. Such influences include family, church, or denomination. Investigators point out, for example, that there is a higher correlation between the beliefs of children and their parents when they are brought up with their parents than between those children who are brought up partly away from their parents. This finding is not in the least surprising and certainly it does not cause any great excitement.

2. The psychophysiological-type theories are involved in

discussions of conversion as a form of brain-washing. Several times in the last two decades it has been argued that the mechanisms of suggestion and brain-washing are operative in large evangelistic campaigns. It has been claimed that in such campaigns certain typical ingredients are often to be found. These include a respected speaker given considerable prestige build-up through the media, who preaches with great fervour, conviction and seeming authority. The meeting is frequently crowded and emotional hymns are sung before and after the address. There may also be bright lights, massed choirs and stirring music, the latter often with a strong rhythmic beat. Such factors taken together, so it is argued, can increase the likelihood of conversion occurring. It was situations such as these which were studied by Dr William Sargant in his books *Battle for the Mind* and *The Mind Possessed*.[1]

There seems little doubt that some of the factors listed above influence the thoughts and actions of those present at such meetings. The extent of such influence remains to be clarified by further studies. So far we are only at the beginning of the task of formulating plausible explanations of just what is happening psychologically in such situations and much work remains to be done. The point remains, however, that the careful study of such factors represents a proper labour for those engaged in the scientific study of behaviour. Christians will be as interested as non-Christians in the outcome of such studies. Not that that can tell us anything about the truth of the religious beliefs acquired through such meetings. On that the psychologist has no more and no less expertise than anyone else. Indeed, it is well to remind ourselves that, as mentioned earlier, Professor Skinner, regarded by many as the arch behaviourist, has said:

'I am in no position to give you a complete account of religion any more than a complete account of anything else. But the whole, the history of comparative religion, shows some light

---

[1] Sargant, W., *Battle for the Mind* (Heinemann, London, 1957); *The Mind Possessed* (Heinemann, London, 1973). See also 'The Physiology of Faith', *British Journal of Psychiatry*, 1969, 115, pp. 505-518.

on why men have composed religions, religious practices, and documents and texts and so on. And that is part of the subject-matter of the science of behaviour.'[2]

Since the psychophysiological theories discussed by Dr Sargant have attracted a good deal of attention and controversy, it may be helpful to pause here long enough to consider them in a little more detail. Dr Sargant sees important similarities between what is happening in the brains of people subjected to various forms of so-called brain-washing and those who are suddenly converted at highly emotional evangelistic meetings. Physical and psychological stresses skilfully applied can indeed produce dramatic changes in behaviour and beliefs. Such behaviour is seen by Sargant as very similar to that occurring at religious meetings of, for example, the snake-handling sects of the Southern States of America. In such cases he notices the same kind of emotional exhaustion leading to heightened suggestibility, and points out how at such times beliefs can most readily be implanted. Here, again, it must be made clear that the Christian who is a psychologist is as concerned to understand the truth of the psychophysiological mechanisms as his non-Christian colleagues. Both, moreover, are equally clear that to understand the mechanisms at that level does not say anything one way or the other about the truth or falsehood of the beliefs that are held at the end of the process. That simple logical point is, perhaps, more readily appreciated if we take a less emotionally loaded example. One day we may understand the psychophysiology of the processes whereby scientists make discoveries and produce theories, or of the processes that occur when mathematicians are working out proofs. In neither case, however, should we attempt to evaluate the truth of the scientist's theory or the validity of the mathematician's proof by hooking him up and studying his brain processes. If we want to judge the truth of what he says we shall examine it in the light of whatever is the appropriate evidence. Likewise one would not attempt to decide whether to accept the account that a particular historian gives of a past event by studying

[2] Skinner, B. F. in the TV programme *Firing Line,* 17 October 1971.

his brain processes. Rather, you would more appropriately ask, 'Where is the relevant evidence which I should consult in order to decide what weight to attach to the conclusions which he reaches?'

3. We have already touched upon Freud's psychodynamic theories,[3] and we shall later see that it may indeed be the case that some of the things that Freud said about the function of gods in the lives of some men may be true. As Christians we do not have any stakes in denying the possible truth of some of these theories. What such theories tell us is mostly about the person who believes in a god, and little about the god in whom he believes. The particular function of religion in the life of an individual does not tell us anything about the existence, or non-existence, of the god in whom he believes, or about the truth or falsehood of statements about the god. Those questions must be settled on other grounds. As we have said, our central concern here is not to evaluate the various accounts of psychological and physiological mechanisms at work in conversion, but rather to ask, How should we relate psychological accounts of religious behaviour to the more familiar and more traditional ones given in religious terms? To do this, let us compare what the Bible has to say about conversion with the psychological accounts.

Biblical accounts of conversion

When one reads the Acts of the Apostles with an open mind it is difficult to see how it can be maintained, as some have, that there is only one genuine type of Christian conversion experience which must always be reported in the same way. What we have is a record of different kinds of people with vastly different backgrounds being brought to faith in Christ through different circumstances, and yet, at the end, all sharing a common faith. To illustrate this consider just a few chapters of the Acts of the Apostles. In chapter 8 there is an account of the conversion of an Ethiopian leader. We find him described as a responsible man (verse 27), as a man on a pilgrimage (verse 27), who is reading the Jewish Scriptures (verse 28), and it is clear, according to his

[3] See above, pp. 42–52.

reported conversation, that he is a man with an attitude of eager-
ness to learn about this new faith (verses 31, 34). Here, then, is a
person with considerable previous knowledge about the God of
the Hebrews combined with a desire for further understanding
and a willingness to make a decision once the issues become clear.

In the following chapter we have the well-known account of
Saul of Tarsus, a man with a very detailed knowledge of Judaism
and the Jewish Scriptures (9:1, 2) and also, one may presume,
with a detailed knowledge of the beliefs of the early Christians
since his recent full-time occupation had been persecuting the
Christian church (verses 1, 2). We could speculate a little that,
since witnessing the martyrdom of Stephen (see Acts 7:58), he
may well have had a mounting conviction of the truth of the
beliefs of these Christians as he pondered the amazing way in
which Stephen died. Saul is then subjected to a very traumatic
experience on the road to Damascus (verse 3), an experience
about which volumes have been written from both the Christian
and the psychological points of view. Whatever the particular
details of Saul's experience, the result was clear; there was a
struggle and then a decision expressed in the famous words, 'Lord,
what wilt thou have me to do?' (verse 6 AV).

In the following chapter we find a man who would today be
described as a Company Commander in the armed services (10:1).
It is clear from verse 2 that he is a religious man, for we are told
that he and his whole family joined in the worship of God. His
attitude appears to have been one of expectancy and, therefore,
we are not surprised that he quickly makes a personal decision
when he is given the opportunity to do so and that he welcomes
further instruction from the apostle Peter (verses 25 ff.). A few
pages further on in the narrative we have an account of a woman
whom we are told is already a worshipper of God (16:14). We are
also told how she sits and talks to her friends or, to be more
colloquial, gossips the gospel (16:13). It would seem that the
apostle Paul joined this little group and shared in their chat and
gossip. Just how often this went on before she became a Christian
we are not told, and it is fruitless to speculate. But it seems clear
that, once she had become acquainted with the truth of the

Christian message, she became a Christian (16:15). The same chapter also contains an example of the kind which today would be described as a sudden conversion, the kind that takes place in extremely stressful and traumatic circumstances. The prison keeper at Philippi, a man about whom we know very little, had in his custody some of the apostles. They had been singing hymns (16:25) and talking with one another. Then, in the middle of the night, there was an earthquake. As a result of this the prison doors were opened and the jailer, expecting his prisoners to escape, was on the point of suicide (verse 27). We are told that in these circumstances the apostle Paul spoke to him of the Lord and that he made an immediate decision (verse 34).

These five episodes illustrate the range of experiences and backgrounds just mentioned. From a psychological point of view there were doubtless a range of psychological processes and mechanisms at work. In all cases, however, the outcome was the same belief in God and faith in Christ. To focus on the psychological aspects of these conversions does not mean that one either ignores or denies that it is the *truth* which grips the mind of the hearer, rather than the stirring of the emotions, which is the prime ingredient in any conversion experience.

What the Bible makes clear is that, for all the diversity of background and circumstances of these conversions, they took place because God acted. For example, in the case of the Ethiopian leader, we are told that *it was the Lord* who directed Philip to go to the Gaza road (Acts 8:26) and that *it was the Spirit* who told Philip, 'Go and join the carriage' (8:29). In the case of Saul, *it was the Lord* who directed him to 'get up and go into the city' (Acts 9:6), *it was the Lord* who gave Ananias his instructions (Acts 9:15) to go and help Saul. The centurion was directed, so we are told, *by an angel of God,* to send for Peter (Acts 10:3), 'and the Holy Spirit fell on all who heard the word' (Acts 10:44 RSV). Of the woman Lydia we are told quite explicitly that *it was the Lord* who 'opened her heart' (Acts 16:14). The point is a simple but profound one. Just as in the Old Testament we read that sinners turn to God only when turned by God (for example in Jeremiah 31:18 ff. and Lamentations 5:21), so in the New Testament the conversion of unbelievers to God is the result of a divine work in them. A man responds to the gospel only because God has first begun to work in him.

Whether, then, we study conversion from the standpoint of the psychologist or from the accounts that are given in the Bible and in other religious documents, it is clear either way that it is at once a profound experience and an extremely complex process. There is a tremendous range of different predisposing factors and accompanying behavioural changes involved in conversion. At this stage he would be a bold psychologist, and I believe one who would have to ignore a considerable amount of the relevant evidence, who would say that there is just one psychological mechanism which can account for all the richness and variety of the experiences and behaviours subsumed under the descriptive word 'conversion'. It should be remembered, of course, as we have indicated earlier, that conversion is not something which is exclusive to the Christian faith, but that there are conversions to other kinds of religious faiths and to various non-religious systems of belief, such as political ones.

Relating the psychological and biblical accounts

We are now ready to ask, How are the biblical accounts of conversion to be related to the accounts offered by psychologists and physiologists? Each account has its own distinctive features. Thus the religious account is an 'actor' account of what is going on. That is to say, it is the account which is given by the person being converted. By comparison, the psychological and physiological accounts may be regarded as 'spectator' accounts. They are given from the particular viewpoint taken by the behavioural scientist. Thus he may be interested in environmental factors which seem to accompany the conversion experience, or in the physiological brain processes occurring at conversion. Both viewpoints focus on the one phenomenon of conversion. Each accepts that there is only *one* set of events to study, but that the one set of events may, for the purposes of analysis and under-standing, be usefully viewed from several different aspects.

By 'aspects' we mean here the psychological, the physiological, the biochemical, and the distinctly personal. Certainly the psychological aspects cannot be dismissed as mere epi-phenomena. The experience of conversion is just as real as the experience of the scientist in reading his measuring instruments. The accounts which derive from studying these different aspects should certainly not be regarded as competitors. An account of the physiological processes underlying behaviour is not in competition with a psychological account of the same event. Neither is the psychological account a competitor with the account which the person converted gives in his own personal and religious language.

Certainly those of us working in the behavioural sciences have learned to welcome the fresh information about one set of events which can be contributed by scientists working in different disciplines. We illustrated this in chapter 2 by reference to the study of learning. We saw how we have learned not to regard our different standpoints as competitors, so that we do not claim exclusive rights to the study of a particular piece of behaviour and say 'hands off' to our physiological or biochemical colleagues. Indeed, we welcome the distinctive contributions which our colleagues' approaches make to the understanding of the one set of events. The point is that within its own language system and at its own level, each account may be regarded as, at least in principle, *exhaustive* (although in practice it will be many, many years before any one of us can really give an exhaustive account of even the simplest behavioural event), but none may claim to be *exclusive*.

Thus the personal account which refers to a personal encounter with God does not have to be 'fitted in' to either the psychological or the physiological or the biochemical account, any more than the psychological account has to be fitted in to the physiological account, or the physiological to the biochemical. In general, we find that the personal account of the event is much more concerned with the personal significance of the event than with the particular psychological, physiological or biochemical mechanism which may have been operative at the time. We shall say more of this in a moment.

A variant of an illustration used by Professor Donald MacKay helps to clarify this point. We could imagine ourselves sitting on the cliffs looking out to sea in the company of a friend who is a competent and enthusiastic physicist, the kind who carries about bits of scientific equipment in the boot of his car. As the sun begins to set, and darkness begins to fall, we see a light flashing out to sea. With his usual enthusiasm, our physicist friend rushes to the boot of his car and starts to take measurements. He tells us of the emission rate of the light, its wave-length, its frequency and various other things, all of which to him, as a physicist, are fascinating and important. For our part, we suddenly begin vaguely to recall the Morse Code which, let us assume, we have learned many years before. It gradually dawns upon us that the lights flashing out to sea are communicating a message which says simply, 'The piece of cliff on which you are sitting is crumbling and will shortly slide into the sea'!

Now, of course, no reference to crumbling or sliding or sea will anywhere be evident in the physicist's account of those lights. At the same time, to ignore this aspect is to ignore what for us, personally, is the most significant aspect of these same events. What I am suggesting, therefore, is that as psychologists and physiologists we are, with regard to religious behaviour, some-what in the same position as the physicist was in regard to the flashing light. Our concern is not necessarily with the personal significance of the events but understanding the mechanisms whereby they take place. And so with religious behaviour, and in particular with religious conversion, their personal significance is what figures most importantly in the religious accounts.

Such personal accounts will include, as indeed do those in the Bible, mention of God as a person, and the Holy Spirit. That is not to suggest that the Holy Spirit can be used as an explanatory concept to fit into a psychological account that we wish to give of religious behaviour. That would be to ignore the important truth that, as Professor Austin Farrer has put it, 'the Holy Spirit is God. He is not to be fitted into any psychological, or for that matter personal, explanation that we choose to give.'[4] The God of the Christian is one who upholds and sustains everything

[4] Farrer, A., *Saving Belief* (Hodder and Stoughton, London, 1964), p. 12.

at all times (Hebrews 1:3). It is extremely important to remember this as we think about the relationship between the scientific, psychological accounts of conversion and the significance of the event to the person who is converted.

The point is that the whole pattern of events which lead up to a man's conversion is to be regarded as given by God. What, therefore, the converted man is asserting is that, to do full justice to the whole of his experience, he finds it necessary to interpret that experience in religious terms. He now sees, if you like, a new pattern in past and present events. A conversation here, a film there, a book, a debate or an argument, a particular religious service, a sermon – all of these are now seen to fit together into a coherent pattern of events so that they make sense at the deepest level only when interpreted in a God-centred framework. In short, his conversion is now most accurately described as entering into a personal relationship with Jesus Christ. The non-Christian can always say, of course, that he finds that particular kind of explanation superfluous, or that kind of interpretation meaningless. As far as I can see, no amount of arguing can ever produce any incontestable proof that the non-Christian is right and that the Christian is wrong, or vice versa. It is not that the Christian has, so to speak, a special set of religious sense receptors which he can tune in to the religious wave-length to pick up information which is not available to the non-Christian. Rather it is that, for the Christian, his experience makes sense to him at the deepest level as personal dialogue between himself and God.

In a sense, there is nothing new in all this. When Jesus Christ himself was upon the earth some regarded him simply as Jesus the man. Others, seeing the same person and observing the same events, came to acknowledge and trust him as Jesus the Christ. On one occasion, John tells us, there was a split amongst the Jews. Many people said, 'He is possessed, he is raving.' Others said, 'No one possessed by an evil spirit could speak like this. Could an evil spirit open blind men's eyes?'[5] The same, presumably, is true today when two people listen to a sermon. There are those who hear of Jesus and begin to see him as Christ and acknowledge

[5] John 10:20, 21.

him as Lord. There are others hearing the same words, utilizing, if you wish, the same psychological processes, yet who continue to see him simply as Jesus the man, the historical figure.

I think it is at this point that it becomes particularly difficult to help those who are not already Christians to appreciate the kind of certainty which the Christian has for his belief in God. C. S. Lewis illustrated this particularly well in one of his sermons which he entitled 'Transposition'.[6] He pointed out how you can imagine a situation in which two friends are listening to a third friend playing, say, Beethoven's Fifth Symphony on the piano. One can imagine this happening in a situation where one of the two friends has heard the symphony played by a full concert orchestra, whilst the other has never heard it played before. As the piano plays on, the first friend keeps chipping in and saying, 'There, did you hear the cellos? that was the flute, that was the clarinet', and so on. And the second friend becomes steadily more irate and protests that he can hear nothing but a piano playing. In one sense, of course, he is perfectly right. But the point is that the first friend, having once heard Beethoven's Fifth with all the added dimensions given to it by a full concert orchestra, thereafter interprets his subsequent experience in the context of those added dimensions. At this point the best thing the first man can do is to invite his friend to accompany him to a full orchestral performance of Beethoven's Fifth. Perhaps this is analogous to the Psalmist's exhortation to 'taste and see that the Lord is good' and to Christ's own promise that 'him who comes to me I will not cast out'. In coming, however, the honest seeker soon finds that there are some searching, and at times painful, issues to be faced up to and dealt with; in other words he discovers that genuine repentance precedes real faith. But that is another story and this is not the place to tell it.

[6] Lewis, C. S., 'Transposition' in *They Asked for a Paper* (Bles, London, 1962), pp. 166–182.

9 Same words, different meanings

Pseudo-conflicts can arise through failing to notice that a word or phrase used in religious writings has a different meaning when used technically by psychologists. In this chapter I shall describe two instances where this has occurred. By examining these in some detail I hope to reduce the likelihood of such unnecessary misunderstandings being perpetuated. If that happens, we shall have brought a little nearer the constructive collaboration in a common cause between psychology and religion which I advocated in chapter 1.

Moral learning and development

Psychologists and those studying the Christian religion are both interested in moral learning and development. Our task here is not to attempt a synopsis of the present state of psychological knowledge of this subject but to see where the interests of the psychologist and the Christian are the same and where they are different. Those who wish to go more fully into the psychological aspects of this may confidently be referred to a recent book *Moral Learning and Development* by Douglas Graham.[1]

When a Christian student at, say, a College of Education hears that the course includes lectures on moral learning and development he naturally thinks of what the Bible teaches about growth towards Christian maturity, of the goal of the Christian to be conformed to the image of Christ and of the progression towards

[1] Graham, D., *Moral Learning and Development* (Batsford, London, 1972).

moral perfection which that implies. When, therefore, after several weeks he has heard no reference to the work of the Holy Spirit, and no statements about 'growth in grace', he is tempted to conclude that his lecturer does not believe in these things. It is true that he may not, but then again he may, and just as fervently as the confused student. But in his lectures he is trying to expound the results of psychological research aimed at identifying those factors which facilitate the development of moral behaviour and those which interfere with it. Once it is agreed what is meant by moral behaviour (and that will differ to some extent from one religion to another and from one culture to another), what factors lead to such behaviour and what impede progress towards it becomes an empirical psychological question. At this point the concerned humanist with his strongly held ethical and moral standards can whole-heartedly collaborate with his Christian colleague in designing and carrying out a programme of psychological research aimed at increasing our understanding of the development of moral behaviour.

How does the psychologist set about studying moral development? He tends to use one or both of two main approaches. He may conduct wide-ranging field studies. For example, he may study the correlations between personality characteristics, methods of early upbringing and the development of moral behaviour. In addition, he may carry out experiments in which he varies things like reward and punishment, their nature and degree, and looks for what effects the different treatments have on subsequent moral behaviour. Studies of this second kind have only been attempted in recent years, but so far, although the picture is still rather confusing, the results are sufficiently encouraging to justify further work along similar lines.

What does one typically conclude from such studies? A quotation from the section on Moral Development in a book widely used by students at British universities will illustrate the answers to that question. In reviewing one group of studies aimed at discovering more about how an adolescent's behaviour is related to his early upbringing, the author writes:

'There is a large measure of agreement among these studies which have compared delinquents with matched non-delinquents for family conditions. On the basis of these studies, the conditions conducive to the development of internalized forms of moral behaviour appear to be these: strong affectional ties between parents and children; firm moral demands made by parents upon the children; the consistent use of sanctions; techniques of punishment that are psychological rather than physical, that is, techniques which signify or threaten withdrawal of love; and a high use of reasoning and explanation. When the affectional ties are very close and exclusive, and when parental demands are impossibly high and withdrawal of love and sanction always used, there is a danger that the child will be neurotically "guilt-ridden". This is especially the case when relations between the parents are strained. By contrast, delinquents tend to come from homes where affectional ties are weak, where parents are erratic and inconsistent (lax one moment and over-strict the next), where punishment tends to take the form of aggressive physical or verbal assault and where little attempt at explanations is made. The relative importance of the roles of mother and father is still unclear; but the evidence suggests that, though the paternal role is important, the maternal role is the more fundamental.'[2]

Much of what is written in this technical psychological jargon will strike the reader as common sense in a new dress. In a way that is true, because in psychology we must often first establish empirically the things we have for long held to be common knowledge. At times such common sense turns out to be anything but sense. And even where our earlier beliefs are confirmed, that, in itself, does not necessarily make it any easier to implement them. As regards the issues raised in the above quotation Christians have as much to learn from such findings as non-Christians. How many of us make 'consistent use of sanctions', or always expend the effort involved in a 'high use of reasoning and explanation'? It is not only non-Christian homes where 'relations between the parents are strained', where 'parents are erratic and inconsistent' and where 'little attempt at explanations is made'. Perhaps we all need the results of such psychological studies to give added reasons for doing more consistently what we know all along we should be doing.

Before leaving this topic of moral development we can with profit use it to illustrate how it is one thing to collect the facts but another to produce a satisfying theoretical framework to explain them.

One psychologist will turn to psychoanalytic theory and will explain his results in terms of the interactions within the personality of the ego, the super-ego and the id. Another, starting from different presuppositions, will formulate a quite different explanation of the same set of data. He may, for example, apply the principles of learning theory to the data on moral learning. In that case he will assume that there is nothing about moral learning to distinguish it from other forms of learning. He may then appeal to an explanation in terms of the development of conditioned anxiety responses or regard the development of resistance to temptation as a form of instrumental learning. Yet another psychologist, wishing to emphasize the importance of social influences but still within a general framework of learning theory, will focus on the processes of social learning operating in interpersonal situations. He will supplement his use of the concepts of conditioning and instrumental learning by reference to imitation and identification. We can illustrate this by a further quotation from D. S. Wright's book. After reviewing the ways in which such theories have been used in the explanation of moral learning and development, he concludes,

'None of the theoretical positions just described seems quite adequate to account for these developed forms of moral behaviour in which all aspects of moral responses are integrated under cortical, or conceptual control. Maturity in moral behaviour presumably involves some kind of creative autonomy, in which the individual modifies his own moral responses in the light of ideas and reasons.'

In short, we have made a start, but there is a long way to go yet. The point remains, however, that when a more adequate and all embracing psychological account of moral learning and development is available, it will not be, and by its nature cannot be, a competitor with that other account, already shared by Christians, couched in terms of man's response to the directives of a loving Father God who, making clear 'the way', invites his children to 'walk in it' as learners or disciples.

In closing this section, then, we must return briefly to the point with which it opened, namely, the need to distinguish between psychological studies of moral development, on the one hand, and personal beliefs based on religious convictions concerning the theory and practice of moral education on the other.

On this, as on other issues, the committed Christian has a position and a standpoint. It is neither neutral nor arbitrary, and is one that can and must be defended rationally and by appeal to the relevant evidence. It is one thing to discover those factors which facilitate the process of developing a pattern of behaviour which more often than not conforms to the moral norms of a particular group or culture. That is important and the Christian applauds all legitimate research directed to increasing our knowledge of such factors. At the same time the Christian will not be satisfied with conformity at the level of overt behaviour alone, important though that is. He will be mindful also of the strand of Christian teaching exemplified in the so-called Sermon on the Mount which takes the matter a stage further and deeper to the level of attitudes and motives.

Guilt, guilt feelings and psychotherapy

We turn now to consider how the same word may have quite different meanings when used in the psychological and religious contexts. Our concern is to make clear that, when rightly understood, the specifically Christian meaning is not to be regarded as a competitor with the psychologist's meaning. One area of converging interests between the psychologist and the Christian in which pseudo-conflicts can readily arise through such confusions of meaning is psychotherapy. This is because at times the same words or phrases are used without distinguishing between the different meanings given to them by the psychotherapist and the theologian or Christian layman. To ignore this difference is to be well set on a collision course between psychology and theology. As an example of how such pseudo-conflicts arise let us consider the word 'guilt'.

Most of the discussions of guilt in the psychological literature arise in a clinical context. There the psychotherapist almost always uses the word as shorthand for 'guilt feelings'. The psychotherapist is not concerned with indicating an objective forensic state, but rather a psychological event or state. A man may feel guilty, but not be guilty of the offence from which his experience of guilt is said to be derived. There is no reason why two distinguishable states, 'feeling guilty' and 'being guilty', should exist in any direct proportion. In fact, in the pathological state, they certainly do not.

By contrast, when the theologian uses the word 'guilt' he is referring to an objective ethical or forensic relation between a man and God. As Christians, moreover, we believe that a man's objective sinful and alienated relation to God, with its attendant effects upon all his relations to his fellow men, normally, when acknowledged, gives rise to a psychological state of valid guilt.

To clarify the difference between psychological guilt and theological guilt, let us consider a hypothetical situation. It is one suggested by Dr Paul Meehl in the Symposium *What then is man?*[3] to illustrate the distinction between the two meanings of the word guilt just referred to. We may imagine (he says) an employee in a particular business who, being less well-off than his employer, finds it all too easy to be envious of him. He experiences feelings of aggression and hostile impulses towards him, together with, at times, almost uncontrollable uncharitable feelings. Not only may he covet his employer's status and his money, but he may also covet his home and his attractive wife. Let us further imagine

---

[3] *What then is man?* (Concordia Publishing House, St Louis, Missouri, 1958).

that, in attempting to cope with all these aggressive and hostile feelings, the employee represses them and finds that he has developed some neurotic symptoms. On a psychodynamic view it would be said that it is his attitude of hostility, partly conscious, but mainly unconscious, which in this case has generated his guilt feelings.

Such a psychodynamic interpretation is not the only possible interpretation and, indeed, it may not be the correct one. For example, it could also be maintained that the guilt feelings are ones that have been learned by a process of conditioning early in life. But the fact remains that the guilt feelings now find themselves associated with these particular aggressive, uncharitable, hostile, envious attitudes. The aim of the psychotherapist is to relieve and if possible to break this neurotic condition. He has the task of restoring the person's psychological integrity. In so far as the patient feels so hostile towards his employer that at times he would like to annihilate him, he is a sinner. In so far as the patient is managing to disguise his wish and its attendant guilt by various symptoms, he is neurotic. It would be a mistake to ask, is the patient a sinner or is he just neurotic? The point is that he is 'both-and' simultaneously. From a theological point of view we say that, in respect of his envy, hostility, covetousness and so on, the man is a sinner, and that he is in a state of objective guilt. By the same token we must also say from theological premises that if he were not a sinner or, if the impossible could happen and he could become utterly sanctified whilst upon earth, then he would not have such thoughts and impulses. Therefore in one sense, it would be literally correct to say that he develops his particular neurotic problem because of his sin. If he were not a sinner he would not be a neurotic. And yet the psychotherapist is certainly not thereby committed, as part of his professional task, to curing sin. This, indeed, would be a function far beyond his province and powers. From a theological point of view, we may legitimately assert that, if sin had not entered the world, there would be no neurosis. But at the same time we must also realize that not all sinners are neurotics. As Dr Meehl has well put it, the secular therapist's job is 'to help a neurotic sinner to become a healthy one'. By health here he means roughly that degree of confidence and gratification and freedom from symptoms which is normal in our society, in short, the norm accepted by most insurance companies as a definition of mental health.

At times the question is raised of whether the psychotherapist, to put it bluntly, is not making the Christian minister redundant. The argument then runs something like this: 'Surely, in so far as the psychotherapist is helping to lessen, remove or restrict guilt feelings, he is alleviating a man's proper conviction of sin and therefore reducing his likelihood of seeking forgiveness in Christ.'

Clearly there is some overlap here in the roles of the psychotherapist and minister. Both are committed to the restoration of the health and happiness of the distressed person. By health here we refer, as mentioned above, to that condition in which the individual is relatively free of medical symptoms and experiences no more frequent or intense anxiety or feelings of guilt than most people do; he also experiences such anxiety and guilt in appropriate contexts and is able to work productively and enjoyably and to experience the normal gratifications in his social, affectional and sexual life. Such a picture of health certainly fulfils the normal medical and social criteria. The basic nature of the contract between a patient and his psychotherapist is simply that the therapist endeavours to assist the patient to a state of health approximating as closely as possible to the one just outlined. But this certainly is not to say that the psychotherapist is in any sense in the missionary business, conceived from a Christian point of view. Indeed, if a client should come to a therapist saying that he wants to get right with God or that he wants to be a more holy person, the therapist should decline to enter into a contract with him. The therapist's job is to help the patient to become healthier and happier: it is not even his job to make him good in the sense of possessing civil righteousness. It is possible, of course, and it often happens, that successful psychotherapy makes a patient morally better even though it is not its avowed aim. By the same token it may also occasionally result inadvertently in the patient being socially or ethically better, although this is most unlikely. On the other hand, it also happens occasionally that, after a course of psychotherapy, a person may not only be more readily able to express his normal sexual impulses but may in addition act generally more aggressively and impulsively.

In principle this presumably should not cause any more concern than the other case cited by Meehl in *What then is man?* of a man whose former occupation was that of a pickpocket and who, having developed a severe tremor of his right arm, was faced with a very serious occupational disability! As Dr Meehl pointed out with reference to this particular case, the neurologist treating such a man may succeed in treating him successfully and, as a result, enable him once again to become an effective crook. Certainly it is the physician's job to restore the man's organic integrity; but it is not his job to reform crooks. Likewise the psychotherapist's task is to heal neurotics, not to convert sinners, or even to reform scoundrels. The point is a simple one. Healthy people are sinners: neurotic people are sinners. If a healthy Christian is tempted to think of his neurotic brother as more sinful than himself, then he is thinking as the Pharisee thought about the publican in Luke 18:9–14. This way of thinking is most dangerous, since it implies a close relationship between a person's degree of sinfulness and the state of his mental health. To state the matter bluntly in this way is not, as some may think, to suggest that the effects of conversion and sanctification should not be felt in experience and shown in behaviour. Certainly, if a neurotic becomes converted, he will be a different neurotic afterwards.

To sum up then. It is easy to see how failure to define the word 'guilt', or any other word that is shared by psychotherapists and others, can quickly lead to false conflicts being generated. We have seen how, when theologians and psychologists both use the same word 'guilt' without making its meaning clear, pseudo-conflicts arise. For example, in the course of treating a neurotic individual, the psychotherapist may say something like 'So-and-so is getting over some of his guilt'. Wrongly interpreted this may be seen as a claim to be doing what the Christian, from a biblical standpoint, knows that only Christ can do. Hence the Christian's understandable concern when the psychotherapist appears to be saying, 'I am removing the guilt', or 'I am convincing him that he has no objective guilt'. The latter statement, however, is precisely what the psychotherapist is not saying. His statements refer purely and simply to 'guilt feelings' and have nothing to say one way or the other about the man's objective state before God. The psychologist, in so far as he is acting as he should do in an ethically neutral way towards his patients, is simply making a sick person healthy. The healthy person remains a sinner, albeit now a healthy sinner, and as such remains guilty before God, unless he seeks and finds forgiveness through faith in Jesus Christ.

10 God: comforting illusion or demanding reality?

In view of the criticisms of Freud's psychological theories, summarized in chapter 3, it could be argued with some justification that it is a waste of time even to consider his views on religion. Since they are widely known, however, and still influential in some circles, I propose to outline them briefly and to indicate where I believe they were in error. I shall also discuss them as an example of a type of psychological explanation claiming to show how psychodynamic theories of personality can account for why people behave religiously. Even though, as I believe, Freud's theories were so wide of the mark, that does not mean that other, more plausible, psychodynamic theories cannot and should not be developed. I shall argue that, whilst such theories have important things to teach us about why men believe in God, they cannot, by their nature, confirm or deny the truth that God exists. Neither can they be used to decide whether God revealed himself historically in the person of Jesus Christ.

That religious beliefs are nothing but wish fulfilment is a view still held by some of those who have read the works of Sigmund Freud and his later disciples. It should be apparent, however, to anyone with more than the most rudimentary knowledge of psychology that such an equation is an over-simplification so great that it does not do justice to the intelligence of a man of Freud's stature. But that does not prevent its being widely believed, particularly by those who, for other reasons, are looking for a way of easily disposing of the more morally demanding claims of the Christian faith. Freud himself was well aware, and was at pains to point out, that some of the key features of his view of religion were not new, and had been held by non-believers in earlier generations. But what his psychoanalytic theories did was to suggest fresh theoretical bases which could provide some new underpinning for these previously held views.

Freud on primitive religion

Freud's views on religion are presented in a series of books. Some of these have been so severely criticized[1] on the basis of their factual inaccuracy that it is not profitable to devote a great deal of time to considering them. Others, however, are more relevant and have more substance in fact to support them.

In *Totem and Taboo*, written in 1913, we find Freud attributing the origin of religion to the psychological connection between the so-called Oedipus complex and totemism as it existed within small primitive groups. Freud had given the name 'Oedipus complex' to the notion of an unconscious hostility which young men have to their fathers, and he supposed that the young men of a primal horde had killed their father in order to possess his wives. According to this theory, he suggested that

> 'the totem feast was the commemoration of the fearful deed from which sprang man's sense of guilt (or original sin) and which was the beginning at once of social organization, of religion and of ethical restriction'.

Whilst this approach seemed to Freud to give some clues to the development of more primitive religions, and particularly those that exhibited early forms of patriarchial totemism, he later developed a somewhat different principle to explain the existence of higher religions.

Before discussing his view of higher religions, we should in fairness note that he was limited by the then existing anthropo-

[1] See, for example, Spinks, G. S., *Psychology and Religion* (Methuen, London, 1963).

logical knowledge. This has increased enormously since 1913 and, in the light of what is now known, it is clear that many of the 'facts' upon which Freud based his theory of the origins of primitive religion were simply wrong. It is not surprising, therefore, that his theory also is wildly misleading, and for this reason it is not profitable to spend more time on this particular view of the origins of religion and ideas of God.

Very similar comments can be made about Freud's book entitled *Moses and Monotheism* (1939) which has been criticized on similar grounds, namely, that factually it is inaccurate. Specifically, his ancient history was wrong, and this is crucial for his whole case. Wilhelm Schmidt[2] makes this clear in his searching critique of the factual basis of Freud's theories. Schmidt lists five serious objections to the view that totemism is the source of all subsequent religions. Spinks[3] has summarized Schmidt's views as follows:

'1. Totemism as a practice does not belong to the earliest forms of human development. Peoples who are ethnologically the oldest have neither totemism nor totemistic sacrifice.

'2. Totemism is not a universal practice. Schmidt adduced substantial evidence to show that three of the leading races of mankind, the Indo-Europeans, the Hamitol Semites, and the Ural Altaics had originally no totemistic practices.

'3. Freud's adoption of Robertson Smith's assumption that the ceremonial killing and eating of the totem animal is an essential feature of totemism is valueless. "Of the many hundred totemic races of the whole earth there are just four who know any rite even approximating to this one and they all belong, ethnologically speaking, to the most modern totemic peoples."

'4. Pre-totemic peoples know nothing about cannibalism, so that the parricidal meal would be an impossibility.

[2] Schmidt, W., *The Origins and Growth of Religion*. Eng. trans. by H. J. Rose (Methuen, London, 1935), pp. 103 ff.
    [3] Spinks, G. S., *op. cit.*, p. 83.

'These four objections, Schmidt summed up in a fifth objection:

'5. "The form of the pre-totemic family, and, therefore of the earliest human family we can hope to know anything about . . . is neither general promiscuity nor group marriage, neither of which, according to the verdict of leading modern ethnologists, ever existed at all." '

Spinks further points out how anthropologists such as Malinowski advanced other serious criticisms of Freud's theories. He writes:

'Culture and religion, said Malinowski, do not spring suddenly into being as the result of a supposed historical event but are slow accumulation of experience. "It is impossible to assume origins of culture as one creative act by which culture, fully armed, springs into being out of one crime, cataclysm or rebellion."[4] There are also criticisms which can be offered on psychological grounds:

' "If the real cause of the Oedipus complex and of culture into the bargain is to be sought in that traumatic act of birth by parricide; if the complex merely survived in the 'race memory of mankind' – then the complex ought obviously to wear out with time. On Freud's theory the Oedipus complex should have been a dreadful reality at first, a haunting memory later, but in the highest culture it should tend to disappear."[5]

'In addition, Malinowski criticized Freud's patrilineal explanation of the origins of religion by comparing such systems with the matrilineal forms of the Trobriand Islanders. In the West patrilineal forms are understandably associated with the Oedipus complex, but matrilineal societies show no feelings of hatred for the father while the infant's feelings for the mother are spontaneous and non-incestuous.'[6]

---

[4] Malinowski, B., *Sex and Repression in Savage Society* (Kegan Paul, London, 1937), p. 167.
[5] *Ibid.,* pp. 167 f.
[6] Spinks, G. S., *op. cit.,* pp. 83 f.

Freud on developed religion

As regards more developed religion, Freud presents us with his views in two shorter books. The first, *The Future of an Illusion*[7] was published in 1927, and the second, *Civilization and its Discontents*[8] appeared in 1930. Freud used the word 'Illusion' to stand for any belief system which was based on human wishes. In doing so he was careful to point out that such a basis did not necessarily imply that the system was false. This is a strange misuse of the term illusion to say the least. As far as Christianity was concerned he did in fact believe that the system was false, not because it was based on wishful thinking but because, as far as he could see, there were no other grounds for supporting it. He certainly did not deny that it had served a useful purpose in that it had provided, in the past, a sense of security for man in the face of a hostile environment and had proved a useful reservoir for ethical standards in the development of civilization. It seemed clear to him, however, that the time had come when such a reservoir could no longer usefully serve the needs of modern man who must replace it by rational grounds for living a civilized life.

Ultimately Freud came to see religion as an interim social neurosis out of which man must grow as he becomes educated to cope with, and be more closely in touch with, reality. He thus emphasized the way in which, in the past, religion has so often offered a means of escape from the harsh realities of life. In the face of the challenges and puzzles of the natural world, and in the face of the constraints imposed upon men by organized society, religion offers, on the one hand, an explanation of the puzzles and, on the other, an escape from the constraints. According to this view religion could help to explain the origin of the universe. It could also give some sort of assurance of protection in this life, a promise of final happiness in a life to come and provide an authoritative discipline for daily living.

Developing the idea of religion as a means of protection and escape, Freud saw the function of gods as substitute ideal fathers. Religion then became the projection of the child's psychical

[7] Freud, S., *The Future of an Illusion* (Hogarth Press, London, 1934).
[8] Freud, S., *Civilization and its Discontents* (Hogarth Press, London, 1939).

relationship with its earthly father so that gods in all the different religions were seen simply as magnified father figures. This is well summed up in Freud's own words which appear in two sentences near the end of his psychological study of Leonardo da Vinci:

'Psychoanalysis has made us aware of the intimate connection between the father complex and the belief in God, and has taught us that the personal God is psychologically nothing other than a magnified father; it shows us every day how young people can lose their religious faith as soon as the father's authority collapses. We recognize the root of religious need as lying in the parental complex.'[9]

This theme of God as the magnified father is one which Freud expressed repeatedly as he described the way in which he believed the mythologies of the world's religions consistently demonstrated that religion itself is 'nothing other than psychological processes projected into the outer world'.

Freud was obviously concerned to explain why so many people practised religion and held religious beliefs. Illusory or not, they were still very widespread. Freud recognized that a system of beliefs which satisfies our needs may be true or false. The fact that it satisfies our needs does not in itself constitute grounds for believing that the system is true nor, for that matter, for believing that it is a workable and comforting illusion. Either way we must look for a more substantial basis for such beliefs. The Christian would certainly wish to maintain that there are good reasons for holding his beliefs and that they are firmly anchored in the historical happenings of the life and teaching of Christ, as well as in the history of the people of Israel and of the Christian church.

Some of Freud's later followers took a much more aggressive and destructive point of view than Freud himself. They seemed to believe that to demonstrate that a belief might be the product of unconscious wishes was in itself adequate grounds for rejecting that belief. Nevertheless, the fact that a belief might be shown to

[9] Freud, S., *Leonardo da Vinci* (Kegan Paul, London, 1932).

have an unconscious origin does not thereby show the belief is untrue. Strangely enough, the adherents of the case against religion based on the grounds that such beliefs are the product of unconscious wishes apparently never realized what a two-edged sword it was. For the psychoanalytic treatment of religious belief as being the product of unconscious wishes can be applied equally well to the treatment of the unbelief of those who wish to refute religion. This point of view has been carefully worked out by Rumke in his small book *The Psychology of Unbelief.*[1]

Other psychodynamic views of religion

Before leaving the psychoanalytic approach to the understanding of religious beliefs and their origins, it is perhaps worth noting that one of Freud's early distinguished collaborators, Jung, developed views of religion totally opposed to those of Freud. Professor Spinks, in the book referred to above, after reviewing both Freud's and Jung's views on religion, concludes that 'for Freud religion was an obsessional neurosis and at no time did he modify that judgment. For Jung it was the absence of religion that was the chief cause of adult psychological disorders. These two sentences indicate how great is the difference between their respective standpoints on religion.' The important point to note here is that any claim that unambiguous deductions concerning the status of religious beliefs can be drawn from psychoanalytic theory is refuted by examining the totally opposed deductions drawn by its two early exponents. Starting from very similar psychoanalytic viewpoints they developed totally different views of the function of religion and of the status of religious beliefs.

Others have developed views of the function of religion and religious beliefs in ways similar to Jung, and have pointed to some of their benefits to mankind. This view was expressed by Flower[2] in 1927 and by Bartlett[3] in his 1950 Riddell Memorial Lectures. Flower suggested that a religious response to a situation may be one way of providing a possible means of bringing that

[1] Rumke, H. C., *The Psychology of Unbelief* (Rockcliff, London, 1952).

[2] Flower, J. C., *An Approach to the Psychology of Religion* (Kegan Paul, London, 1927).

[3] Bartlett, F. C., *Religion as Experience, Belief, Action* (OUP, London, 1950).

situation under control. Bartlett, in similar vein, saw religion as a way of helping to make sense of the world and providing a basis for coherent action, especially when it is necessary to go beyond the immediately available evidence in taking such action. It is apparent that these and other views share the common thread that religion is in some way a means of dealing with the problems and frustrations of life, and this in turn often results in the construction of an imaginary world in order to meet these frustrations.

Michael Argyle, in two of his books,[4] examines the extent to which the available empirical evidence supports this and other hypotheses about the function of religion. For example, he finds some support for the view that religion is a fantasy gratification and a way of meeting frustration and satisfying needs. This is seen in the increasing otherworldliness of the beliefs of some of the smaller sects, whose adherents come largely from the lower social economic classes. Put bluntly, if you lack this world's goods, you emphasize their transience and the virtues of concentrating your energies on the rewards of a world to come. That there are other reactions to frustration than religious adherence is evident, however, from the hippie cult today.

Since Argyle put forward his views we have witnessed the proliferation of such hippie cults. It is evident that many of those who join them come from affluent middle-class American families, and certainly did not lack this world's goods. Nevertheless, they renounce material things and choose to live in primitive economic conditions. This is one response to frustration. Another is to turn to exotic Eastern religions where it is hoped the satisfaction denied them by material things alone will be found. For these religion may again be a response to frustration. Now, however, it arises not from lack of this world's goods, but because such things have been tried and found wanting. All this underlines the extreme complexity of the roots of religious behaviour and should warn against the uncritical acceptance of any one psychological explanation of such behaviour claiming to deal comprehensively with so diverse a subject.

[4] Argyle, M., *Religious Behaviour* (Routledge, London, 1958) and Argyle, M. and Beit-Hallahmi, B., *The Social Psychology of Religion* (Routledge, London, 1975).

Readers who are interested in weighing the available evidence for and against these and other psychological theories purporting to give account of the functions of religion are recommended to read Argyle's books just referred to.

Skinner on God and religion

Before leaving this topic a contemporary view of the psychological function of religion which has recently received wide publicity must be briefly considered. It is a view propounded by Professor Skinner whose contribution to experimental psychology is, as we have noted earlier, widely taught in university psychology courses. In his book *Beyond Freedom and Dignity* he describes what he believes are some of the important wider implications of his scientific findings, and in the process examines religious beliefs and practices through his reinforcement-tinted spectacles. He believes he can see how his principles of learning, based on the effects of rewards and punishments, can afford yet another explanation of the way in which the practices of religion function psychologically. In his own words:

'A religious agency is a special form of government under which "good" and "bad" become "pious" and "sinful". Contingencies involving positive and negative reinforcement, often of the most extreme sort, are codified – for example as commandments – and maintained by specialists, usually with the support of ceremonies, rituals and stories.'[5]

When he was questioned about these views he commented,

'I think that the good, whether represented, personified in a god does represent those things which we find, to use a technical term, reinforcing. They're the things which induce us to behave in certain ways and evil – well the ordinary Christian picture of Hell is a collection of all the aversive stimuli available at the time. It did not have electric shock because it was not available. But these are the things.'[6]

[5] Skinner, B. F., *Beyond Freedom and Dignity*, p. 116.
[6] Skinner, B. F. From the TV programme *Firing Line*, 17 October 1971, p. 4.

Moreover, when he was pressed to indicate how such a psychological account of the maintenance of religious behaviour and the functional significance of ideas of God was related, according to his model, to traditional talk about belief in God, Skinner asserted that he was translating notions of God into contingencies of reinforcement and similar jargon. Thus he claimed that, when listening to someone talking about God, he 'ran a translation inside'. The translation was from 'God talk' to what he regards as the original version from which such talk is derived, the original version being statements in terms of schedules of reinforcement. Thus he says:

> 'As to the translation I wasn't translating in the way in which you thought. I was trying to go back to what I took to be the original version of which, to my mind, theories of God are translations. I think men have evolved a conception of God in some sense to represent the good, which I think can be reduced to what we find as positively reinforcing. And they have conceptualized the devil or evil to take care of aversive stimuli in general.'[7]

We should note, however, that, in the way Skinner appeared to be using the word God, it was a fundamental logical mistake to regard one statement as simply a translation of the other. They were not translations; but they were correlates. Moreover, Skinner's contention that he is doing no more than translating becomes less convincing when one notices how, in the very act of explaining what he means by a translation, he speaks of concepts of God being 'reduced to' what we find positively reinforcing, *etc.*

The point is that any account that Skinner might wish to give of the maintenance of religious behaviour or ideas of God, simply adds to the set of psychological explanations of religious behaviour. Thus to talk about reinforcements as Skinner does, at a mechanistic level, is yet another psychological explanation and has the same logical status as talk about the ego, the super-ego and the id, or about nerve nets and reverberating brain circuits. These

[7] From the transcript of *Firing Line*, p. 5.

are not simply translations of what people say when they talk either about other people or about God. To argue in the way that Skinner appears to do is thus once again to commit the fallacy of 'nothing-buttery'. As MacKay pointed out in the discussion with Skinner, just quoted from, what Skinner is saying is tantamount to asserting that a 'No smoking' sign is nothing but ink on cardboard and therefore it is perfectly all right to go on smoking. It is like saying that what is going on in a computer when it is solving a mathematical equation is nothing but electronics. Mathematicians watching the computer would quite rightly assert that they were watching the solution of a particular mathematical equation and they would find it odd to hear it suggested that they were merely making 'translations' of what the electronic engineer might say in electronic terms. To press the analogy further, MacKay suggested that it would be rather like someone writing a book called *Beyond Mathematics* on the grounds that he had now discovered how to make a 'translation' of all the things mathematicians ever wish to say in terms of electronic concepts concerning the working of his computer without any mention of mathematical concepts. If he were to do this he would just simply be laughed out of court by mathematicians.

The immediate point of relevance here is that, just as no-one is wishing to deny that it is a proper pursuit for the electronic engineer to describe in electronic terms how the computer solves mathematical equations, neither is one wishing to deny that it is proper for the psychologist to look for psychological accounts of how a man comes to know God. The psychological account can no more be presented as a refutation of the reality of the God whom the person has come to know, than can the electronic account be presented as demonstrating that mathematical concepts are now redundant and superseded.

Evaluating psychological accounts of the function of religion

It is quite understandable for a Christian to over-react to analyses and interpretations of the function of religion and the origin of religious beliefs such as I have just outlined. He feels, intuitively, even if he cannot at once put his finger on the logical fallacies and unjustified psychological extrapolations spelled out above, that such criticisms indicate very inadequate and distorted views of the God he worships. They are caricatures of the God he has met in Christ and who has down the ages authenticated himself and his servants in 'many mighty acts'. At the same time not all the psychological accounts of how religious beliefs and practices function in the lives of individuals and groups are linked with anti-religious philosophies. And even those that are can be separated out from their philosophical framework and judged on their psychological merits. When one does this it may enable one profitably to take stock of one's faith from a different viewpoint. For example, one may ask oneself to what extent one's religious faith may be functioning exclusively, or almost exclusively as an escape mechanism, rather than in the balanced way in which it is presented in the Bible. No-one who takes the whole of the Bible seriously and studies its emphasis on the outgoing nature of a living faith in God can accept an escapist version of Christianity as normative. How can one describe as escapists the champions of the history of Israel and the first Christian believers who were so outgoing that they could be said to be turning the world upside down? No-one who pays attention to such evidence can be satisfied with a form of religion which becomes escapism, nor with a belief system so preoccupied with subtle theological points that it misses the main impact, teaching and challenge of the doctrine of the incarnation.

It would make an interesting study to follow through the ways in which heretical Christian views have arisen whenever men have been more controlled by what they needed their faith to say than by what in fact God has revealed in the Bible. This, of course, is one very important reason why some of us believe that it is essential to take seriously what God has revealed to us in the past and what is preserved for us in Scripture. Here is a template against which we can continually test our beliefs, especially when they seem to be becoming more controlled by what we want them to say, or what we want God to be like, than by what in fact he has said and has revealed himself as being like.

It seems clear, then, that nothing is to be gained by denying that belief in God functions differently for different people, as well as differently for the same people at different times. Allport, in his book *The Individual and his Religion: a Psychological Interpretation*, illustrates this clearly as he discusses the ways in which religion develops from youth to adolescence and through into maturity.[8] His account is substantiated with a large amount of empirical evidence gathered from the psychological study of religion and religious behaviour. Those who wish to follow out the details of this evidence are referred to Allport's book and to Argyle's book *Religious Behaviour*.[9]

Not only do beliefs function differently for the same people at different times, but it also seems clear that people with personalities which differ because of inherited characteristics, as well as the formative influence of early environment, may reflect their personality differences in the relative importance which they attach to the grounds which they find support their religious beliefs most strongly. Professor Thouless expounds some of these grounds for religious belief in detail.[1] Here we can do no more than simply note them in passing. Firstly, there are those who formulate their beliefs in terms of certain intellectual formulae and who find intellectual satisfaction and rational elegance in the way in which their religious beliefs make sense of the totality of their experience. There are others who would lay much greater emphasis upon the emotional basis of their religious beliefs. It is certainly true that in many religions, emotions and feelings are intimately involved, and in some cases deliberately cultivated by artificial means. For this reason some investigators have seized upon these as a means of identifying something unique about the function of religion. On closer scrutiny, however, it soon becomes apparent that the emotions which are most often talked about in the context of religion are also experienced in other, quite clearly non-religious contexts. For example, the emotions most often

[8] Allport, G. W., *The Individual and his Religion: a Psychological Interpretation* (Constable, London, 1951), p. 67.

[9] Argyle, M., *op. cit.,* p. 148.

[1] Thouless, R. H., *An Introduction to the Psychology of Religion*, 3rd ed. (CUP, London, 1971), p. 7.

talked about in this respect include those which a person experiences as he is confronted by the more striking and awesome phenomena of nature. His feelings at moments when new insights into some aspect of life are achieved are also regarded as particularly significant.

Such experiences and feelings, however, have ready counterparts in many situations which would not normally be regarded as religious. It is difficult, therefore, to see how they alone help to define the function of religion in any unique way. Amongst research scientists, for example, it is well known that, when a new insight is gained on an issue which has been a puzzle for a long time, there may be accompanying strong feelings of elation and intense pleasure. Those who doubt this should read a book like Coulson's *Science and Christian Belief,*[2] or Beveridge's *The Art of Scientific Investigation.*[3] Or again we may note the way in which in recent years the feelings sometimes associated with religious or mystical states have been sought by the use of various psychotropic drugs. The relevant point here is simply that the search for feeling states which can uniquely define the function of religion is not very promising and is a very unsure foundation for religious beliefs.

Summing up

This chapter has done no more than give examples of the kinds of psychological explanations which have been offered for how the idea of god arose and of the psychological functions of religious beliefs. That some of these may, when we understand them better and can refine them more, turn out to be true, should not surprise us and certainly should not worry us. At the risk of becoming tedious in repeating it, we must make it clear that the fact that a belief may satisfy a need or stem partly from an unconscious wish, neither validates nor invalidates the belief in question. Its truth or falsehood will have to be determined in each case in the light of the relevant evidence. We shall not decide whether Jesus lived

---

[2] Coulson, C. A., *Science and Christian Belief* (Fontana, London, 1967).
[3] Beveridge, W. I. B., *The Art of Scientific Investigation* (The Scientific Book Club, London, 1955).

2,000 years ago by seeking to attribute the origins of that belief today to some repressed unconscious wish. We shall decide the truth or falsehood of that by studying the relevant historical evidence which is there for all to see.

In this respect it is noteworthy that the essence of the Christian revelation is conveyed to us in terms of a person, that is, of Jesus Christ, who was truly man and truly God; that the core of the Christian message is conveyed to us in terms of a relationship, a relationship of love between a father and a son. We are not surprised to learn, therefore, that just as human relationships have different significances and different emphases at different times and in different situations, so the implications of our sonship to our heavenly Father have different significances, different emphases and different implications at different times in our life. Indeed, anyone who chooses to study the Bible at all carefully soon discovers that the same God who expressed himself and his relation to his children as that of a Father, at other times expressed his relationship in different terms, such as that of a Creator or a Judge. At times he speaks with sternness, at times with rebuke, and at other times with compassion and tenderness. But the underlying theme which pervades all these different aspects of his relationship is that of a strong, unchanging and unwavering love for man, which means that man can fully depend upon God.

Is God, then, nothing more than a fantasy father figure? For some people he may be; in which case that will tell us something interesting about the person who holds that belief. But it certainly will not tell us anything about the existence of God. If we are looking for an answer to that question we shall not find it by studying the psychological differences between people in the way in which they hold their religious beliefs. Rather we shall find the answer to that question by examining the evidence with a critical and open mind, with a readiness to be confronted with the truth when it, or as we would prefer to say he, is presented to us.

11 Looking back and looking forward

Looking back: conflicts to be avoided

Psychologists have developed skills to apply in solving a quite remarkably wide range of problems. Specialization within psychology has already progressed to a point where, at times, two psychologists find it quite difficult to communicate. One, studying the biochemistry of motivations, may have little interest in, or understanding of, what motivates a teenager. The psycho-pharmacologist's language will be almost incomprehensible to the social or developmental psychologist. At times they may even be tempted to regard one another as competitors. A little thought soon reveals, however, that they are allies in a common cause – the understanding of man, his behaviour and experience. But religious people also have a very keen interest in what makes people tick. This shared interest has at times generated fruitless conflicts rather than productive co-operation in a common cause. In examining some past conflicts I have tried to bring out what distinguishes the scientific psychological approach from the religious approach.

Not all conflicts have arisen because of a failure to define the specific and deliberately limited objectives of scientific psychology. At times conflicts have arisen because of a failure to distinguish between, on the one hand, the reasonably well assured findings of scientific psychology and, on the other hand, the speculations and claims of pre-scientific psychology. Thus, the speculations of Freud and the early psychoanalysts were too readily embraced as being well established and secure scientific findings. As a result unnecessary conflicts arose. Or again, more recently, some of the extrapolations and speculations of writers like Desmond Morris in *The Naked Ape* and B. F. Skinner in *Beyond Freedom and Dignity* have been confused with the scientific basis from which they are unjustifiably claimed to be derived. It is easy, of course, to be wise after the event, and it will always be difficult to distinguish between psychological findings which are reasonably securely anchored in empirical data and those which are more speculative. Nevertheless, it is essential that the effort should be made to assess the factual basis of any claims made in the name of psychology before rushing in to generate conflicts between such findings and Christian beliefs.

We also saw how important it was to distinguish between the models of contemporary psychology and other complementary models used in other approaches to the study of man. We noted how necessary it was to distinguish between the models of man used by scientific psychologists and those appropriate to the study of man through art, literature and religion. Each in their own way are equally valid. Each contributes its distinctive account. Together they deepen our understanding of the mystery of man and his behaviour. In the past, however, false antitheses have been set up between the models of man used by scientific psychologists and the models of man given through Christian revelation. In this regard, we noticed how important it was to distinguish between the different meanings given to words common to the vocabulary of psychology and theology. The word 'guilt' was a case in point. We also saw how important it was to recognize the different aims of the psychologist and the religious adherent in trying to understand religious behaviour. We noticed that the principal emphasis in Scripture, for example, is not on the psychological mechanisms whereby conversion takes place, but the fact that it is God who is responsible through and through for a man's conversion.

Our examination of the peculiar properties of scientific and religious explanations emphasized how important it was to differentiate between exhaustive and exclusive explanations of behaviour. The psychologist seeks to produce, within his own particular area of specialization, an account of behaviour at that particular level. In principle such an account may be or may become exhaustive. That does not confer any exclusive right, however, to its being the only relevant or important explanation. We saw that within psychology itself we recognize the need for exhaustive accounts at several different levels. None of these can claim to be exclusive. Equally, when all the exhaustive accounts at the mechanistic scientific level have been offered, it does not justify a claim that they are the only ones exclusively worthy of consideration. This confusion between exhaustive accounts and exclusive accounts was exemplified over and over again, and we recognized it each time as another illustration of what we termed 'nothing-buttery'.

Looking forward: allies or enemies?

The problems we face today are much too serious to be allowed to become a source of contention between men of good will who share a common concern for the welfare of mankind. The challenge to face such problems must unite men, not divide them. The seriousness of the challenge was highlighted at the close of the 1969 International Conference of Psychology when a symposium was held entitled *Psychology in the Future*.[1] The Chairman, Dr George Miller, said on that occasion:

'What, then, is the context of contemporary psychology? It must be obvious to anyone who reads the newspapers that we are today, all over the world, sorely beset by a whole spectrum of social problems that must be solved if civilized society, as we know it, is going to survive ... our most pressing problems today are social problems – problems that we have made for ourselves – and their solutions will require us to change the ways we behave in our personal and institutional context. Psychology, as one of the sciences of behaviour, should have much to contribute to such a problem and so is more likely than some other sciences to be subjected to social pressures arising outside of psychology itself.'

[1] *Psychology in the Future*. A symposium published by the International Union of Psychological Science and the British Psychological Society, 1971.

The Christian, who is a psychologist, will be doubly motivated to share in meeting this challenge. As a psychologist he will want to direct his particular training and skills towards the solution of specific problems. As a Christian he will see his work as one way of expressing his love for his brother and fulfilling Christ's commands. At the same time he will be under no illusion that man's basic spiritual problem, which stems from a deep-lying attitude of rebellion against God and his claims upon men, can be dealt with by psychological techniques alone, be they ever so sophisticated. To believe that would be to perpetuate the error of Teilhard de Chardin and his belief in man's continuing ascent to perfection. As we have pointed out elsewhere,[2] that kind of outlook finds men otherwise so diverse in outlook as Julian Huxley and Teilhard de Chardin unitedly trying to 'infuse with new hope and new blood a pessimistic world'. A world that

' . . . has become so afraid of the atomic bomb that in desperation it grasps eagerly at this new gospel which promises that after all there is an optimistic end for all of us without any reference whatever to the gracious activity of God. For such a view', says Hooykaas, ' . . . propounds an optimistic world view, which compensates for the disappointment about the hard reality of life by an apocalyptic vision of a rosy future, allegedly based on a purely scientific foundation. This is perhaps the reason of its rapid spread, for modern Man is willing to swallow any kind of opiate if it is presented to him in the name of Science.'[3]

Two other distinguished contributors to the symposium *Psychology in the Future* quite independently drew attention to a topic hitherto largely foreign to contemporary psychological writings, namely, the power of love. Dr Karl Pribram and Professor Harry Kay both referred to the need for a new understanding of the nature and the power of love. Dr Pribram said,

[2] Jeeves, M. A., *The Scientific Enterprise and Christian Faith* (Tyndale Press, London, 1968), pp. 110–113.
[3] Hooykaas, R., 'Teilhardism, A Pseudo-Scientific Delusion' in *The Free University Quarterly*, Vol. 9, 1, 1963, p. 1.

'But we know so little about the skill of love: the strategies and tactics of making love recur and endure; this is the challenge to tomorrow's psychology.'[4]

And Professor Kay commented,

'Psychology will gain much in understanding when it takes a more positive approach and examines man's virtues as well as his vices. We have had so few studies of loyalties and affections, his ideas of veracity and kindliness. Harlow's famous address on "The Nature of Love" (1958) was more than a remarkable *tour de force*; it was the beginning of several experimental programmes, both in the laboratory and natural field, which have served to establish the complexity and ramification of these first expressions of succour and security. We need many more such research programmes.'[5]

It is good to hear this public recognition of a dimension to man's living hitherto so studiously avoided by most psychologists. At the same time, unless the word 'love' is carefully defined when put to use in psychological theories, and is distinguished from its unique usage in Christian theology, a good deal of confusion and pseudo-conflict could easily arise. With such immense problems facing us that would be a tragedy. So long as the distinctive contributions that true faith and true science can make to the solution of such common problems are borne in mind, conflicts need not arise.

The Christian can never be satisfied with tackling these problems only at what might be called the horizontal level. Christianity, rightly understood, must by its very nature bring in an entirely new dimension, a dimension desperately needed in the pessimistic world in which we live today. This dimension is the hope that comes as one recognizes, as we saw in chapter 4, that man is a

[4] Pribram, K., 'Psychology Tomorrow: The Immediate Future' in *Psychology in the Future*, p. 7.
[5] Kay, H., 'Psychology – A.D. 2000: Facts, Forecasting, Fantasies and Fallacies' in *Psychology in the Future*, p. 10.

creature belonging to God, made by God, redeemed by God, and still loved by God. If Christians ever stop proclaiming the uniqueness and vital importance of this vertical dimension to love, and content themselves with spelling out its implications for the horizontal relationship of man to man, then they will have abdicated their distinctive calling.

It seems to me, then, that at this point Christians must emphasize their distinctive contribution to the solution of man's present dilemma. There is steady pressure to water down the uniqueness of the Christian message so that it looks as much like current popular ideologies as possible. Of course, Christians can, should, and do share with their humanist colleagues the need for men to show a new understanding of one another, a new compassion, a new practical concern for the well-being of one another. But this is not enough. To stop at that is to be sub-Christian. And one must add that, even to a sympathetic onlooker, a good deal that passes as Christian in, for example, the training of men for the ministry of the Christian church today seems to be, at times, anything but Christian.

For example, one gets the impression that men are more and more being trained to act as amateur social workers, sociologists, psychologists, psychotherapists, social administrators, marriage guidance counsellors and so on, as if this were the *primary* calling of the Christian minister. With so much professional training available for those who wish to enter these callings, the Christian minister should make up his mind whether he is called primarily to proclaim the unique message of the Christian faith, or to be a social worker, marriage guidance counsellor, or what have you. I have the impression that some, who as young men felt called to the ministry of the church, have begun to lose confidence in the power of the gospel. As a result they have tended more and more to fill in their time with other activities. One can sympathize with their feelings. The solution, however, or so it seems to me, is to recapture their confidence in their Lord and renew their energies to present him and his love for men with a fresh clarity and a new urgency, *not* to add to the numbers of amateur practitioners of one or more of a variety of social agencies.

The Christian, then, recognizes the need for a renewed emphasis on love between men; but his love springs, in the first place, from his recognition of God's love for him. It is God's initiative which has gripped and captivated his mind and his heart. The outward expression of this love is to be seen in his endeavour to be like the one in and through whom pre-eminently this love was expressed, that is the Lord Jesus Christ himself. The standard and the motive for the Christian is the love of Christ. It is his love which is to motivate us, and we must measure ourselves by no lesser standards than his standards, not by those of other people.

In short, we must be preoccupied with God and the love that he has shown in Christ. Such a preoccupation will, incidentally, meet the demands made by the third contributor to this same symposium, *Psychology in the Future*. Dr Masanao Toda of Japan identified a problem which, he believes, is in the more distant future going to become of unprecedented proportions. It is the problem of finding an entirely new social system and way of life *which can bring back to men a new sense of purpose*. Thus, he wrote,

'One of the symptoms is the prevailing feeling of purposeless-ness among the younger generation in highly energized societies, indicating a lack of ideologies and beliefs strong enough to absorb their energies.'[6]

And he adds, a little later on,

'One of the central problems with which the psychologist is going to have to grapple is that of ways of knowing man better, knowing what really makes him tick.'[7]

Here again, as Christians, we must insist that, when the last word has been spoken by us, as scientific psychologists, about what really makes man tick, there remains something even more fundamental to be said. This is that man was made by God, in his

---

[6] Toda Masanao, 'Possible Roles of Psychology in the Very Distant Future' in *Psychology in the Future*, p. 20.
[7] *Ibid.*, p. 20.

own image, and for the purposes of God. Without this dimension, the pessimism seen today amongst some scientists and others is understandable. But the Christian can have no part in this pessimism, for he knows that 'all things work together for good for those who love God and are called according to his purpose' (Romans 8:28), and that 'the One who started the good work in you will bring it to completion by the Day of Christ Jesus' (Philippians 1:6).

Index of biblical references

Author index

Subject index